# Academic Encounters

## 2nd Edition

**Miriam Espeseth**
**Series Editor: Bernard Seal**

**Human Behavior** **4**

**LISTENING**

**SPEAKING**

CAMBRIDGE
UNIVERSITY PRESS

# CAMBRIDGE
## UNIVERSITY PRESS

University Printing House, Cambridge CB2 8BS, United Kingdom

One Liberty Plaza, 20th Floor, New York, NY 10006, USA

477 Williamstown Road, Port Melbourne, VIC 3207, Australia

314–321, 3rd Floor, Plot 3, Splendor Forum, Jasola District Centre, New Delhi – 110025, India

79 Anson Road, #06–04/06, Singapore 079906

Cambridge University Press is part of the University of Cambridge.

It furthers the University's mission by disseminating knowledge in the pursuit of education, learning and research at the highest international levels of excellence.

www.cambridge.org
Information on this title: www.cambridge.org/9781108348294

First published 2004
Second edition 2012
20  19  18  17  16  15  14  13  12  11  10 9 8 7 6 5 4

Printed in Great Britain by CPI Group (UK) Ltd, Croydon CR0 4YY

*A catalogue record for this publication is available from the British Library*

*Library of Congress Cataloging in Publication Data*

Espeseth, Miriam.
[Academic listening encounters]
Academic encounters, human behavior, level 4 : listening and speaking / Miriam Espeseth. — 2nd ed.
p. cm. — (Academic encounters. Human behavior)
"Audio production: John Marshall Media. Video production: Steadman Productions"—T.p. verso.
Previous ed.: 2004.
Includes index.
ISBN 978-1-107-60298-4 (Student's book with DVD)
1. English language—Textbooks for foreign speakers. 2. Human behavior--Problems, exercises, etc.
3. Listening—Problems, exercises, etc. 4. Readers—Human behavior.
5. English language--Sound recordings for foreign speakers. I. Title.

PE1128.E83 2012
428.2'4—dc23

2012012504

ISBN 978-1-108-34829-4 Student's Book with Integrated Digital Learning
ISBN 978-1-107-60301-1 Teacher's Manual

Additional resources for this publication at www.cambridge.org/academicencounters

Art direction, book design, and photo research: Integra
Layout services: Integra
Audio production: John Marshall Media
Video production: Steadman Productions

# Table of Contents

# Scope and Sequence

## Unit 1: Mind, Body, and Health • 1

| | Content | **L** Listening Skills | **S** Speaking Skills |
|---|---|---|---|
| **Chapter 1**<br><br>**The Influence of Mind over Body**<br><br>page 3 | **Interview 1**<br>The Stress of Teaching First-Graders<br>**Interview 2**<br>The Stress of Being a Police Officer<br>**Lecture**<br>Stress and the Immune System | Following directions<br>Listening for specific information<br>Listening for tone of voice<br>Drawing inferences | Predicting the content<br>Personalizing the topic<br>Comparing information from different sources<br>Asking for opinions<br>Sharing your cultural perspective |
| **Chapter 2**<br><br>**Lifestyle and Health**<br><br>page 20 | **Interview 1**<br>Starting Smoking and Trying to Quit<br>**Interview 2**<br>Quitting Smoking and How It Changes Your Life<br>**Lecture**<br>Risk Factors in Cardiovascular Disease | Following directions<br>Anticipating answers<br>Drawing inferences | Recalling what you already know<br>Predicting the content<br>Combining information from different sources<br>Asking for confirmation<br>Sharing your cultural perspective |

## Unit 2: Development Through Life • 45

| | Content | **L** Listening Skills | **S** Speaking Skills |
|---|---|---|---|
| **Chapter 3**<br><br>**The Teen Years**<br><br>page 47 | **Interview 1**<br>Being a Teenager in a Different Culture<br>**Interview 2**<br>Starting a New Life in One's Teens<br>**Lecture**<br>Erik Erikson's Fifth Stage of Psychosocial Development: Adolescence | Recording numbers<br>Listening for specific information<br>Completing multiple-choice items<br>Uses of *like* in casual speech<br>Correcting or expressing a negative politely | Examining graphics<br>Using background information to make predictions<br>Reviewing predictions<br>Summarizing what you have heard<br>Combining information from different sources<br>Sharing your cultural perspective |
| **Chapter 4**<br><br>**Adulthood**<br><br>page 65 | **Survey**<br>The Best Age to Be<br>**Lecture**<br>Developmental Tasks of Early Adulthood | Recording numbers<br>Summarizing what you have heard<br>Uses of *get*<br>Listening for specific information | Predicting the content<br>Responding to true/false statements<br>Identifying who said what<br>Sharing your personal perspective<br>Eliciting a conclusion<br>Applying general concepts to specific data<br>Sharing your personal and cultural perspective |

| **V** Vocabulary Skills | **N** Note Taking Skills | Learning Outcomes |
|---|---|---|
| Reading and thinking about the topic<br>Examining vocabulary in context<br>Building background knowledge on the topic<br>Breaking down words to guess their meaning<br>Guessing vocabulary from context<br>Learning words as they are used | Summarizing data<br>Using telegraphic language<br>Summarizing what you have heard | Prepare and deliver an oral presentation on health and healthy habits |
| Reading and thinking about the topic<br>Examining vocabulary in context<br>Building background knowledge on the topic<br>Guessing vocabulary from context | Paraphrasing what you have heard<br>Using symbols and abbreviations<br>Outlining practice | |

| **V** Vocabulary Skills | **N** Note Taking Skills | Learning Outcomes |
|---|---|---|
| Reading and thinking about the topic<br>Examining vocabulary in context<br>Building background knowledge on the topic<br>Guessing vocabulary from context<br>Considering different perspectives | Using space to show organizational structure<br>Organizational structure | Prepare and deliver an oral presentation on a particular period of life |
| Reading and thinking about the topic<br>Examining vocabulary in context<br>Building background knowledge on the topic<br>Guessing vocabulary from context | Creating a chart<br>Paying attention to signal words | |

| V Vocabulary Skills | N Note Taking Skills | Learning Outcomes |
|---|---|---|
| Reading and thinking about the topic<br>Examining vocabulary in context<br>Guessing vocabulary from context | Restating what you have heard<br>Mapping | Prepare and deliver an oral presentation comparing body language in two cultures |
| Reading and thinking about the topic<br>Examining vocabulary in context<br>Guessing vocabulary from context<br>Comparing information from different sources | Recording information<br>Reading nonverbal cues<br>Recalling what you already know<br>Summarizing what you have heard | |

| V Vocabulary Skills | N Note Taking Skills | Learning Outcomes |
|---|---|---|
| Reading and thinking about the topic<br>Examining vocabulary in context<br>Describing a typical scene and activities<br>Reminiscing about a typical scene and activities<br>Building background knowledge on the topic: Culture notes<br>Building background knowledge on the topic: Statistics on friendship<br>Guessing vocabulary from context | Recalling what you already know<br>Summarizing what you have heard<br>Using morphology, context, and nonverbal cues to guess meaning | Prepare and deliver an oral presentation on a famous friendship or love relationship |
| Reading and thinking about the topic<br>Examining vocabulary in context<br>Building background knowledge on the topic<br>Guessing vocabulary from context | Conducting a survey using the Likert scale<br>Taking advantage of rhetorical questions<br>Outlining Practice | |

# *Academic Encounters:* Preparing Students for Academic Coursework

## The Series

*Academic Encounters* is a sustained content-based series for English language learners preparing to study college-level subject matter in English. The goal of the series is to expose students to the types of texts and tasks that they will encounter in their academic coursework and provide them with the skills to be successful when that encounter occurs.

## Academic Content

At each level in the series, there are two thematically paired books. One is an academic reading and writing skills book, in which students encounter readings that are based on authentic academic texts. In this book, students are given the skills to understand texts and respond to them in writing. The reading and writing book is paired with an academic listening and speaking skills book, in which students encounter discussion and lecture material specially prepared by experts in their field. In this book, students learn how to take notes from a lecture, participate in discussions, and prepare short presentations.

## Flexibility

The books at each level may be used as stand-alone reading and writing books or listening and speaking books. They may also be used together to create a complete four-skills course. This is made possible because the content of each book at each level is very closely related. Each unit and chapter, for example, has the same title and deals with similar content, so that teachers can easily focus on different skills, but the same content, as they toggle from one book to the other. Additionally, if the books are taught together, when students are presented with the culminating unit writing or speaking assignment, they will have a rich and varied supply of reading and lecture material to draw on.

# A Sustained Content Approach

A sustained content approach teaches language through the study of subject matter from one or two related academic content areas. This approach simulates the experience of university courses and better prepares students for academic study.

## Students benefit from a sustained content approach

**Real-world academic language and skills**
Students learn how to understand and use academic language because they are studying actual academic content.

**An authentic, intensive experience**
By immersing students in the language of a single academic discipline, sustained content helps prepare them for the rigor of later coursework.

**Natural recycling of language**
Because a sustained content course focuses on a particular academic discipline, concepts and language recur. As students progress through the course, their ability to work with authentic language improves dramatically.

**Knowledge of common academic content**
When students work with content from the most popular university courses, they gain real knowledge of these academic disciplines. This helps them to be more successful when they move on to later coursework.

## The Content Areas of *Academic Encounters*

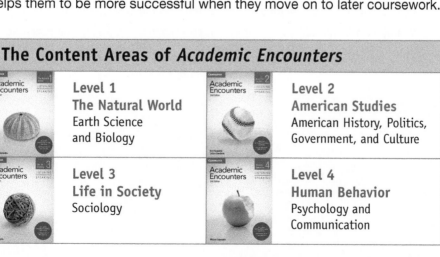

**Level 1**
**The Natural World**
Earth Science
and Biology

**Level 2**
**American Studies**
American History, Politics,
Government, and Culture

**Level 3**
**Life in Society**
Sociology

**Level 4**
**Human Behavior**
Psychology and
Communication

# Academic Skills

*Academic Encounters, Listening and Speaking* teaches skills in 4 main areas. A set of icons highlights which skills are practiced in each exercise.

## L Listening Skills

The listening skills tasks are designed to help students develop strategies before listening, while listening, and after listening.

## S Speaking Skills

Students learn how to participate in formal and informal situations at universities, including sharing opinions, presenting research, and creating extended oral presentations. These skills and tasks were carefully selected to prepare students for university study.

## V Vocabulary Skills

Vocabulary learning is an essential part of academic preparation. Tasks throughout the books focus on particular sets of vocabulary that are important for reading in a particular subject area as well as vocabulary from the Academic Word List.

## N Note Taking Skills

In order to succeed in university courses, students need to be able to take notes effectively. Each unit teaches a range of note taking skills, ranging from organizational strategies and listening for key numbers to using your notes to prepare for tests.

# Preparing for Authentic Listening

## 3 Recording numbers 🅛 🅢

Many listening tasks involve understanding numbers and writing them down quickly.

🔊 **A** Study the empty graph, where you will record growth rates for James and Sarah. Then listen and follow the speaker's directions.

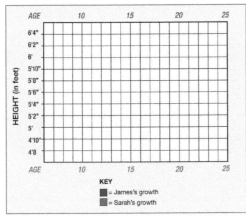

**KEY**
- ■ = James's growth
- ■ = Sarah's growth

**B** Work with a partner. One of you will describe James's growth rate, and then the other will describe Sarah's. As you listen to your partner, check that you have the same information on your graph.

**C** Try to remember your own adolescent height changes and describe them to your partner. Were you ever much taller or much shorter than your peers?

> Students develop a range of **skills** to help them **anticipate and prepare** for the listening tasks.

---

**INTERVIEW 3** Airi: Touch

## 1 Examining vocabulary in context 🅥

Here are some words and expressions from the interview with Airi, printed in **bold** and given in the context in which you will hear them. They are followed by definitions.

**Young Japanese family**

My family **would** never hug him: would + *verb expresses a habitual action in the past*

[not] hug him . . . **much less** kiss: *expresses a very strong negative – stronger than another negative in the same sentence [in this case, hug]*

I**'ve come to** understand his feelings: *have gone through a process of change, and as a result*

**Little by little**, I began to feel: *gradually, over time*

**It's rubbed off on** you: *it's changed [you] gradually over time so that now you like it [informal]*

She **was** just **accepted** to nursing school: *had one's application for admission [as to an academic or training program] approved*

## 2 Summarizing what you have heard 🅛 🅝 🅢

🔊 **A** As you listen to Airi, complete the summary by filling in the blanks. Listen again if you need to.

Airi says that most Japanese people _____ hug and kiss one another. Her American husband felt _____ by this at first: He thought his wife's family didn't _____ . When Airi and her _____ moved to the United States, she was _____ at first because her American family _____ . But now she _____ .

Recently, Airi visited Japan. When she met an old friend, she _____ . The friend looked _____ .

**B** Compare your completed summaries with a partner. You do not need to have exactly the same words.

> The first listenings are **authentic interviews**, in which students develop **listening skills such as summarizing.**

# Academic Listening and Speaking

**A** Read the following advice from the same medical pamphlet on stress (see page 6):

---

**How to Deal with Stress** · · · · · · · · · · · · · · · · · · · · · · · · · ·

_____ Become part of a support system: Let your friends or co-workers help you when you are under too much stress and try to help them, too.

_____ Think positively: Don't worry about things that may not happen. If you do, your mind will send negative signals to your body.

_____ Anticipate stressful situations: If you know that you will be in a stressful situation, plan what you will do and say.

_____ Take care of your health: Exercise regularly, eat well, and get enough sleep.

_____ Make time for yourself: Every day, take some time – even if it's just a few minutes – to be alone, to relax, to do something just for yourself.

---

**B** Which of the suggestions from the pamphlet does Nancy follow? Write N next to these. Which ones does Sam or the LAPD follow? Write S next to these. Compare answers with a partner and discuss any differences.

## 2 Drawing inferences ⓛ

> When you listen to people speak, you must not only think about what they tell you directly but also be aware of what they communicate indirectly. Drawing inferences, or gathering information beyond what a speaker actually says, is a critical aspect of listening.

**A** Read the following statements about the interviews that you heard. Write whether you agree (A) or disagree (D) with each statement.

___ **1.** Nancy is probably in her early thirties.
___ **2.** She takes her job very seriously.
___ **3.** She doesn't teach during the summer.
___ **4.** She enjoys her work as a teacher.
___ **5.** Sam is probably in his forties.
___ **6.** Patrol officers probably experience less illness than supervisors.
___ **7.** Sam likes being a police officer.

**B** Work with a partner. Check to see if you drew the same inferences. Explain why you wrote what you did. You may disagree about some of the statements.

---

**Post-listening activities** help students **analyze and understand** the authentic inverviews.

---

**Students then study and practice using discrete speaking skills, as they express their own opinions about the academic content.**

---

## 3 In Your Own Voice

In this section, you will discuss and conduct research on smoking and other habits that affect your health.

Answer the questions below:

**1.** Do you smoke now? _____ If yes, have you ever tried to quit? _____
**2.** If no, have you ever been a smoker? _____
**3.** Do you have friends or family members who smoke now? _____ If yes, has that person ever tried to quit? _____
**4.** Do you have friends or family members who have quit smoking? _____

### Asking for confirmation Ⓢ ⓛ Ⓝ

> Asking for confirmation is a very important skill in a foreign language. When someone tells you something and you want to be sure that you understood her correctly, repeat the key words that you heard or paraphrase them, and use question intonation (rising voice). This tactic has an added advantage: It slows down the conversation a little so that you can follow it more easily.

**A** You are going to share your answers in Step A with another student. But first, listen to how the interviewer asks Pat for confirmation as she is interviewing him about smoking. Pay attention to her intonation.

---

**Expressions used by the interviewer to ask for confirmation of what she heard**

I understand that you used to smoke. Is that correct?
So, now, you started smoking when you were about 13, and you smoked for 25 years, did you say?
Back to the cigarettes, huh?
A heart attack!?
Do you mean you've never been tempted to start smoking again?

---

# Academic Lectures and Note Taking

## 4 Academic Listening and Note Taking

In this section, you will hear and take notes on a two-part lecture given by Susan Jenkins, PhD, a licensed clinical psychologist who works primarily with adolescents. The title of the lecture is "Erik Erikson's Fifth Stage of Psychosocial Development: Adolescence." Dr. Jenkins will discuss the challenges that adolescents face, and some ways in which those challenges have changed in recent years.

**BEFORE THE LECTURE**

### 1 Building background knowledge on the topic V S

**A** Dr. Jenkins had her students look up Erik Erikson online. Read the information that one student found, then answer the questions with a partner. Look up any words that are unfamiliar.

> **Psychologist Erik Erikson** (1902–1994) believed that personality develops in a series of eight stages. Erikson's theory describes the impact of social experience across the whole life span.
>
> One of the main elements of Erikson's psychosocial stage theory is the development of ego identity. Ego identity is the conscious sense of self that we develop through social interaction. According to Erikson, our ego identity is constantly changing due to new experience and information that we acquire in our daily interactions with others.
>
> In addition to ego identity, each stage in Erikson's theory is concerned with becoming competent in an area of life. If the stage is handled well, the person will feel a sense of mastery. If the stage is managed poorly, the person will emerge with a sense of inadequacy.
>
> Erik Erikson

1. According to Erikson, how do people develop a sense of who they are (i.e., an ego identity)?
2. Erikson theorized eight stages of psychosocial development. What work does a person have to do at each stage?
3. According to Erikson, what happens if a person does not succeed in doing this work at a particular stage?

The lectures come from transcripts of **authentic university classes**, and are available online, providing students with a fully **immersive academic experience**.

Each unit provides extensive instruction and practice in **taking notes**, helping **students succeed** in university courses.

l. area or topic that one is focusing on
m. happening at the same time and in the same place as; during
n. parts of a whole; aspects
o. concerning things rather than feelings or ideas; part of the physical realm

### 2 Organizational structure N L

**A** The following is an incomplete set of student notes for Part 1 of the lecture. The student has indented to give visual clues to the organization and content. Read the notes and notice how the lecture is organized. Try to predict what you might write in the blanks.

> Lecture pt 1 – Adolescence: ID vs. role confusion
>
> (adolesc = age _____)
> Primary work = _____
>   If unable? → "role _____"
>     = cannot make _____, know what _____
> Components of adolesc work
>   Challenge: phys & genital _____
>     -Confusing for _____ because bodies _____
>     -Rapid _____ e.g., _____ (15.24 cm) in _____
>     Result: adolesc very very _____
>   Same time: social pressure from self and _____ to '_____'
>     = establish _____,
>     think beyond _____
>     keep basic trust: "I can _____"
>     Big challenge – many kids _____ ("hit the wall")
>   Material _____ = choose _____
>     Many kids postpone: _____
>     BUT – most adolescs feel _____ about _____
>   Falling in _____ → _____ ID
>     Very _____ aspect at this period
>     Related to _____ ID because adolesc faces new _____.
>     Dramatic change – can be wonderful or _____ - but always _____

**B** Now watch or listen to Part 1 of the lecture. Take notes on your own paper or computer. Remember to use symbols and abbreviations, and indent as the lecturer moves from the general to the specific.

**C** Use your notes to complete the student notes in the box; then compare your completed notes on this page with a partner. They do not have to be identical.

Academic lectures take place in real college classrooms, complete with interactions between professors and students.

**Chapter 3** *The Teen Years* 61

# Academic Vocabulary and Oral Presentations

## Unit 1 Academic Vocabulary Review

This section reviews the vocabulary from Chapters 1 and 2. Some of the words that you needed to learn to understand the content of this unit are specific to the topics of health and illness – what we might call *technical terms*. Other words belong to the standard Academic Word List used worldwide: They appear across different academic fields and are extremely useful for all students to know. We will call these terms *general academic vocabulary*. They are the focus of this review. For a complete list of all the Academic Word List words in this book, see the Appendix on pages 181-182.

### 1 Word forms

Read the sentences and fill in the blanks with a form of the word. For verbs, use the correct tense and person. For nouns, use the correct number (singular or plural). Note: You will not use all of the word forms given.

1. **to analyze, analysis, analytic:**
   The research group performed an _____ of immune functioning in rats.
   The research group _____ the rats' responses to different stimuli.

2. **to depress, depressive, depression:**
   Stress appears to have a _____ effect on the immune system.
   Stress can _____ the immune system.

3. **environment, environmental, environmentally:**
   One's physical _____ plays an important role in health.
   Two examples of _____ stressors are loud noise and bright lights.

4. **medical, medicine, medication, to medicate:**
   People with high blood pressure benefit from taking a combination of _____ .
   Obesity is a serious _____ problem.
   Doctors are trained to practice _____ .

5. **relevant, relevance:**
   The issue of stress-induced illness has _____ for all of us.
   Psychoneuroimmunology is _____ particularly to people under great stress.

6. **unpredictable, unpredictability, predictable, predictability, to predict:**
   When stress is _____ , it causes damage to the immune system.
   When we cannot _____ when something bad will happen, our systems are more likely to be hurt by stress.
   The _____ of stress increases its negative effects.
   _____ stress is less of a problem for the immune system.

7. **complex, complexity:**
   The _____ of obesity makes it very difficult to treat.

8. **isolation, to isolate, isolated:**
   A person who is socially _____ may be at greater risk for certain health problems.
   Social _____ may contribute indirectly to cardiovascular disease.

> Academic vocabulary development is **critical to student success.** Each unit includes **intensive vocabulary practice**, including words from the Academic Word List.

## Oral Presentation

In this section, you will have the opportunity to educate your classmates about your own culture's body language by comparing it with that of another culture with which you are familiar.

### BEFORE THE PRESENTATION

#### 1 Deciding on a topic

You are going to compare and contrast your own culture's body language with that of another culture, so choose another culture that you know well, and be prepared to do some further research on it if needed. Do not try to cover all of the areas of body language (i.e., facial expressions, gestures, body movement, eye contact, proxemics, and touch). Rather, choose two or three areas that you feel most qualified to discuss.

#### 2 Gathering information

**A** When you have decided what aspects of nonverbal communication to talk about and which cultures to compare, review what you already know. You may want to use a brainstorming grid like the one below.

| Body Language | My Culture | _____ |
|---|---|---|
| Proxemics | People stand close together – esp. couples | |
| Gestures | | |

**B** Now gather additional information to complete your notes by observing people in a public place or by watching videos or TV.

#### 3 Preparing your presentation

Your presentation will compare and contrast the body language of the two cultures that you are presenting. Review the language that you used to make comparisons in Chapter 6 (page 112). Remember to include examples. Write your main ideas on note cards and practice giving your presentation in the mirror or for a classmate.

Central Park in New York City. A public park is a great place to observe body language.

> Students create **oral presentations**, applying the vocabulary and academic content they study in each unit, and **preparing them to speak in a university classroom.**

# To the student

Welcome to *Academic Encounters 4 Listening and Speaking: Human Behavior*!

The *Academic Encounters* series gets its name because in this series you will *encounter*, or meet, the kinds of *academic* texts (lectures and readings), *academic* language (grammar and vocabulary), and *academic* tasks (taking tests, writing papers, and giving presentations) that you will encounter when you study an academic subject area in English. The goal of the series, therefore, is to prepare you for that encounter.

The approach of *Academic Encounters 4 Listening and Speaking: Human Behavior* may be different from what you are used to in your English studies. In this book, you are asked to study an academic subject area and be responsible for learning that information, in the same way as you might study in a college or university course. You will find that as you study this information, you will at the same time improve your English language proficiency and develop the skills that you will need to be successful when you come to study in your own academic subject area in English.

In *Academic Encounters 4 Listening and Speaking: Human Behavior,* for example, you will learn:

- what to listen for in academic lectures
- how to think critically about what you have heard
- how to participate in conversations and more formal discussions
- how to give oral presentations in an academic style
- methods of preparing for tests
- strategies for dealing with new vocabulary
- note-taking and study techniques

This course is designed to help you study in English in *any* subject matter. However, because during the study of this book, you will learn a lot of new information about research findings and theories related to human behavior, you may feel that by the end you have enough background information to one day take and be successful in an introductory course in psychology or communications in English.

We certainly hope that you find *Academic Encounters 4 Listening and Speaking: Human Behavior* useful. We also hope that you will find it to be enjoyable. It is important to remember that the most successful learning takes place when you enjoy what you are studying and find it interesting.

# Author's acknowledgments

At Cambridge, thanks are due first of all to *Academic Encounters* series editor Bernard Seal for involving me in the first edition of *Academic Listening Encounters*. The process of creating the second edition has brought me in contact with many helpful and talented people at CUP; I would especially like to thank the patient and gifted Christopher Sol Cruz and my wonderful editor Maya Lazarus.

In Seattle, my gratitude to all who contributed the interviews and lectures that form the heart of the course. Special thanks also to Ed Rankin, Airi Lowe, JiSook Han, JiSoo Kim, and Gina Panattoni.

*Miriam Espeseth*

# Publisher's acknowledgments

The first edition of *Academic Encounters* has been used by many teachers in many institutions all around the world. Over the years, countless instructors have passed on feedback about the series, all of which has proven invaluable in helping to direct the vision for the second edition. More formally, a number of reviewers also provided us with a detailed analysis of the series, and we are especially grateful for their insights. We would therefore like to extend particular thanks to the following instructors:

Matthew Gordon Ray Courtney, The University of Auckland, New Zealand

Nancy Hamadou, Pima Community College – West Campus, Tucson, AZ

Yoneko Kanaoka, Hawaii English Language Program at the University of Hawaii at Manoa; Honolulu, Hawaii

Margaret V. Layton, University of Nevada, Reno, Nevada

Dot MacKenzie, Kuwait University, Sabah Al-Salem University City, Kuwait

Jennifer Wharton, Leeward Community College, Pearl City, Hawaii

# Unit 1
# Mind, Body, and Health

In this unit, you will hear people discuss health and how it can be affected by different factors, including job stress and smoking. Chapter 1 deals with the way in which the mind affects the body. You will hear interviews with a teacher and a police officer, and a lecture on research concerning the link between our mental and physical states. Chapter 2, on staying healthy, includes interviews with two former smokers and a lecture on how to keep your heart healthy.

# Contents

In Unit 1, you will listen to and speak about the following topics.

| Chapter 1<br>The Influence of Mind over Body | Chapter 2<br>Lifestyle and Health |
|---|---|
| **Interview 1**<br>The Stress of Teaching First-Graders<br><br>**Interview 2**<br>The Stress of Being a Police Officer<br><br>**Lecture**<br>Stress and the Immune System | **Interview 1**<br>Starting Smoking and Trying to Quit<br><br>**Interview 2**<br>Quitting Smoking and How It Changes Your Life<br><br>**Lecture**<br>Risk Factors in Cardiovascular Disease |

# Skills

In Unit 1, you will practice the following skills.

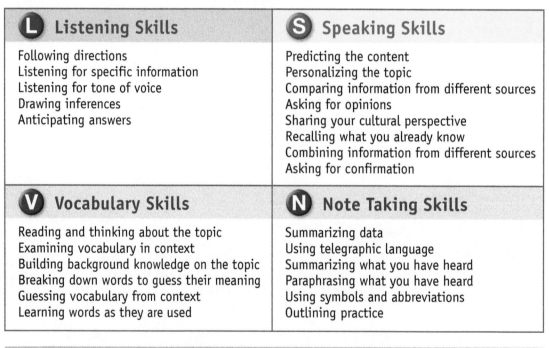

| **L** Listening Skills | **S** Speaking Skills |
|---|---|
| Following directions<br>Listening for specific information<br>Listening for tone of voice<br>Drawing inferences<br>Anticipating answers | Predicting the content<br>Personalizing the topic<br>Comparing information from different sources<br>Asking for opinions<br>Sharing your cultural perspective<br>Recalling what you already know<br>Combining information from different sources<br>Asking for confirmation |
| **V** Vocabulary Skills | **N** Note Taking Skills |
| Reading and thinking about the topic<br>Examining vocabulary in context<br>Building background knowledge on the topic<br>Breaking down words to guess their meaning<br>Guessing vocabulary from context<br>Learning words as they are used | Summarizing data<br>Using telegraphic language<br>Summarizing what you have heard<br>Paraphrasing what you have heard<br>Using symbols and abbreviations<br>Outlining practice |

## Learning Outcomes

**Prepare** and **deliver** an oral presentation on health and healthy habits

# Chapter 1
# The Influence of Mind over Body

Look at the woman above and answer the questions with a partner.

1. Why is this woman so upset?
2. Can you imagine what she is saying right now?

## 1 Getting Started

The focus of this chapter is "Mind over Body" – how our thoughts can affect how we feel physically. In this section, you will begin to examine the topic of stress and how it affects our bodies.

### 1 Reading and thinking about the topic Ⓥ Ⓢ

If you have already read or thought about a topic before you hear it discussed, you will find the discussion much easier to understand.

**A** Read the following passage:

It seems clear that our mental attitude affects the way we feel. One good example of this concerns stress. Stress is an inescapable part of modern life. There are many different causes of stress. Some are minor daily hassles, such as waiting in line or getting stuck in traffic jams. Other stressors can be major life events, such as a death in the family or a divorce. Studies have shown that stress can hurt the body's immune system, resulting in more frequent illness. People who are under a great deal of stress need to learn to cope with and relieve their stress in order to stay healthy.

**B** Answer the following questions according to the information in the passage:

1. What are some major and minor life events that can cause stress?
2. How does stress cause illness?
3. What should someone under stress learn to do?

**C** Discuss your own experiences and opinions with a partner.

1. Can you think of some other sources of stress not mentioned in the passage? Name as many as you can.
2. Do you believe that people under stress are more likely to get sick than those who are not under stress?
3. Can you think of some ways to relieve stress?

## 2 Following directions ⓛ ⓢ

Many everyday listening activities do not require you to speak, write, or remember information for later use. Instead, you simply follow directions.

◀ŋ **A** Listen to some familiar sounds. Follow the speaker's directions.

| Very relaxed | Relaxed | Neutral | Stressed | Very stressed |

**B** Compare your reactions with a small group of classmates.

1. What sounds did you hear?
2. Which sounds did everyone find stressful? relaxing?
3. How did the stress-causing sounds affect you physically? That is, where in your body did you feel them?
4. Which sounds did you and your classmates react differently to? Talk about the reasons for your different reactions.

# 2 Real-Life Voices

In this section, you will hear interviews with two people with very stressful jobs: Nancy, a first-grade teacher, and Sam, an officer with the Los Angeles Police Department (LAPD).

**BEFORE THE INTERVIEWS**

## Predicting the content

> In any listening context, thinking about and trying to predict what you will hear before you listen can greatly increase your comprehension.

**A** Why would it be stressful to be an elementary school teacher? a police officer? Think about it and write your ideas in the boxes.

| Teaching children is stressful because: | Being a police officer is stressful because: |
| --- | --- |
|  |  |

**B** Share ideas as a class. If you hear new ideas, add them to your lists.

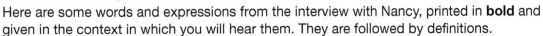

**INTERVIEW 1**  The Stress of Teaching First-Graders

## 1 Examining vocabulary in context

Here are some words and expressions from the interview with Nancy, printed in **bold** and given in the context in which you will hear them. They are followed by definitions.

trying to teach a new **concept**: *idea*

There's a **disruptive** child: *causing problems; behaving badly*

It pulls everyone **off track**: *away from the work that is being done*

things that are in the **curriculum**: *material that must be learned at a specific grade level*

**How** does the stress **manifest itself**?: *What are the signs or symptoms?*

**Fatigue**!: *feeling of being very tired*

The younger the children . . . , the more energy **they require**: *the teacher must have*

I have to **keep my temper** in the classroom: *not become angry*

**Definitely**!: *absolutely, certainly* [strong yes]

Stress does make you **more susceptible to illness**: *likely to get sick more easily and more often*

It weakens your **immune system**: *body's defenses against illness*

## 2 Personalizing the topic ⓢ ⓛ

> Thinking about your own experiences and ideas related to a topic before listening can help you understand and remember the information you hear.

**A** How stressed are you? The following list is from a medical pamphlet on stress. It describes frequent signs of too much stress. Read the list. Write an X in front of any symptoms that you are currently experiencing.

### Frequent Signs of Too Much Stress

_____ Problems eating or sleeping ☐

_____ Increased boredom and great fatigue ☐

_____ Problems making decisions ☐

_____ Increased feelings of anger when small things go wrong ☐

_____ Frequent headaches, backaches, muscle aches, stomach problems ☐

_____ Frequent colds and infections ☐

**B** Now listen. Place a check (✓) in the box after the stress symptoms that Nancy has.

**C** Compare answers as a class.

## 3 Listening for specific information ⓛ ⓝ ⓢ

> Listening for specific information is a useful skill for almost every kind of listening task. Whether we are in the classroom, on the phone, or watching the news on TV, we usually listen for specific information, not for every word.

**A** Read the following questions. Answer as many as you can from your first listening.

1. How long has Nancy taught, and at what levels?
2. Why is teaching more stressful than other jobs, in her opinion?
3. Nancy says that she is sometimes impatient with her own child. Why?
4. What two reasons does Nancy give to explain why she is often sick?
5. What are two things that Nancy does to relieve her stress?

Elementary school teacher

🔊 **B** Now you will hear the interview again. Try to listen for the specific information that you need in order to complete your answers in Step A. Then finish writing your answers.

**C** Compare answers with a partner.

# 1 Examining vocabulary in context ⓥ

Here are some words and expressions from the interview with Sam, printed in **bold** and given in the context in which you will hear them. They are followed by definitions. Note: You may have already heard some of these expressions used in different contexts.

different types of **assignments**: *specific tasks that are part of a person's job*

**the force**: *the police force; the police as a group*

**patrol**: *an assignment in which a police officer walks, bicycles, or drives around a certain neighborhood*

a **traffic violation**: *something illegal that is done by a driver*

More police officers are **injured**: *physically hurt*

a **routine** stop: *regular; not special or unusual*

**ulcers**: *holes in the lining of the stomach that are made worse by stress*

It's **documented**: *shown to be a fact by research; proven to be true*

keep a relationship **at its peak**: *in very good condition; very healthy*

The routine traffic stop

## 2 Listening for specific information Ⓛ Ⓝ Ⓢ

**A** Read the following questions before you listen to the interview with Sam:

1. How long has Sam been a police officer?
2. What does Sam consider the most stressful assignment, and why?
3. What does Sam say about illness on the police force?
4. What programs does the LAPD have to help officers cope with job stress?
5. How does Sam deal with his stress?

**B** Now listen to the interview. Listen specifically for answers to the questions in Step A. Write short answers.

**C** Compare answers with a partner and then with the class. Listen again if you need to.

## 3 Listening for tone of voice Ⓛ Ⓢ

Oral communication comprises much more than simply words and their meanings. An estimated 60 percent to 90 percent of communication is *extralinguistic*, or "outside" of the "words" we use. For example, it is important to pay attention to a speaker's tone of voice. Is he serious? Is he joking?

**A** Read the incomplete statements below. Then listen to short excerpts from the interviews with Nancy and Sam and circle the letter to complete the statements.

1. Nancy sounds _____ of what she is saying.
   a. completely certain    b. somewhat certain    c. very doubtful

2. Nancy sounds _____ of what she is saying.
   a. completely certain    b. somewhat certain    c. very doubtful

3. Sam uses his voice to show that he is _____ what he is saying.
   a. serious about    b. amused by    c. angry about

4. The interviewer is _____ by what Sam says.
   a. bored    b. surprised    c. confused

**B** Compare answers as a class. Listen again if you need to.

**AFTER THE INTERVIEWS**

## 1 Comparing information from different sources Ⓢ

Whether you are reading or listening, one way to deepen your understanding of a topic is to compare information from different sources.

**A** Read the following advice from the same medical pamphlet on stress (see page 6):

**How to Deal with Stress** • • • • • • • • • • • • • • • • • • • • • • • •

_____ Become part of a support system: Let your friends or co-workers help you when you are under too much stress and try to help them, too.

_____ Think positively: Don't worry about things that may not happen. If you do, your mind will send negative signals to your body.

_____ Anticipate stressful situations: If you know that you will be in a stressful situation, plan what you will do and say.

_____ Take care of your health: Exercise regularly, eat well, and get enough sleep.

_____ Make time for yourself: Every day, take some time – even if it's just a few minutes – to be alone, to relax, to do something just for yourself.

**B** Which of the suggestions from the pamphlet does Nancy follow? Write N next to these. Which ones does Sam or the LAPD follow? Write S next to these. Compare answers with a partner and discuss any differences.

# 2 Drawing inferences Ⓛ

When you listen to people speak, you must not only think about what they tell you directly but also be aware of what they communicate indirectly. Drawing inferences, or gathering information beyond what a speaker actually says, is a critical aspect of listening.

**A** Read the following statements about the interviews that you heard. Write whether you agree (A) or disagree (D) with each statement.

___ **1.** Nancy is probably in her early thirties.

___ **2.** She takes her job very seriously.

___ **3.** She doesn't teach during the summer.

___ **4.** She enjoys her work as a teacher.

___ **5.** Sam is probably in his forties.

___ **6.** Patrol officers probably experience less illness than supervisors.

___ **7.** Sam likes being a police officer.

**B** Work with a partner. Check to see if you drew the same inferences. Explain why you wrote what you did. You may disagree about some of the statements.

# 3 In Your Own Voice

In this section, you will conduct some research of your own on work and stress.

## 1 Asking for opinions Ⓢ Ⓛ Ⓝ

> The ability to ask for opinions is not only essential for academic discussion; it is also an excellent way to get people to talk to you.

**A** As a class, list five jobs you think are stressful – including your present job: being an English student. Write them on the board and here. The order is not important.

English student ( ), _____ ( ), _____ ( ),

_____ ( ), _____ ( )

**B** By yourself, rank the five jobs in Step A according to how stressful you think they are. Write the order in the parentheses ( ), using 1 for least stressful and 5 for most stressful.

**C** The language in the box will help you ask a classmate for his or her opinion. First, let's hear the interviewer ask Nancy and Sam for their opinions. Listen carefully to how the interviewer uses her voice when asking for an opinion.

| Language Used by the Interviewer to Ask for Opinions | |
|---|---|
| **Introducing the topic:** | **Asking the specific question:** |
| I'd like your opinion. | Which job would you consider more stressful, _____ or _____? |
| I'm curious to know what you think. | What do you think is the most stressful job anyone could have? |
| May I get your opinion? | What kind of work do you think causes the most stress? |

| Some Additional Ways to Ask for Opinions | |
|---|---|
| **Introducing the topic:** | **Asking the specific question:** |
| I'm interested in your opinion. | Which job do you think would be more stressful, _____ or _____? |
| If you don't mind, I'd like your opinion. | What would you imagine is the most stressful job in the world? |
| May I ask you what you think? | What kind of work do you consider the most stress-causing? |

**D** Using your class's list from Step A and the phrases in Step C, work with a partner. Ask your partner questions to find out how he/she would order the five stressful jobs on your list. For example:

*May I get your opinion? Which job do you think is more stressful, being a police officer or being an English student?*

**E** Complete the first two columns under "Our Opinions" in the table. Enter your partner's opinions from your discussion in Step D in the first column and your own opinions from Step B in the second column.

| Job Ranking[1] | Our Opinions | | |
|---|---|---|---|
| | My Partner's | Mine | My Class's |
| 1. | | | |
| 2. | | | |
| 3. | | | |
| 4. | | | |
| 5. | | | |

1. Rank from least stressful (1) to most stressful (5).

## 2 Summarizing data Ⓝ Ⓢ

Objective information from a group of people, such as a list of rank-ordered items, can be meaningfully summarized by simply adding up the ranking values.

As a class, report the numeric value that each of you assigned to the five jobs in Step E. Then add the numbers to determine which job the class considers the most stressful (highest total), the next-most stressful, and so forth. For example, in a class of 10 students: if 5 students rank "English student" as the *most* stressful job (5 x 5) and 5 students rank it as the *least* stressful job (5 x 1), the total value for "English student" is 25 + 5 = 30. Record the class's ranking in the last column of your table above.

# 4 Academic Listening and Note Taking

In this section, you will hear and take notes on a two-part lecture given by Ellen Cash, a professor of psychology. The title of the lecture is "Stress and the Immune System." Professor Cash will present research supporting the idea that the mind affects the body.

## 1 Building background knowledge on the topic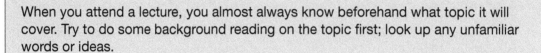

> When you attend a lecture, you almost always know beforehand what topic it will cover. Try to do some background reading on the topic first; look up any unfamiliar words or ideas.

**A** Read the description of the lecture from Professor Cash's course syllabus online:

### Week 4: Stress and the Immune System

- Psychosomatic disorders
- Animal and human research
- Classical conditioning ("Pavlov's dog")
- Implications for health care

**B** In the first bullet above, the word *psychosomatic* may not be familiar. Try dividing it into two parts; look up each part of the word in a dictionary and write its meaning.

*psycho-* = _____

*-somatic* = _____

Can you guess what is meant by "psychosomatic disorders"? Compare guesses with a classmate and check with your teacher for confirmation.

**C** According to the lecture description, Professor Cash will talk about "classical conditioning ('Pavlov's dog')." Let's do some background reading on classical conditioning.

> Classical conditioning was first identified by Ivan Pavlov in the salivation reflex of dogs. Salivation is an *unconditioned response* to food; food is an *unconditioned stimulus*. Pavlov conditioned dogs over time to salivate merely to the sound of a bell (a *conditioned stimulus*) by ringing the bell at the same time that food (an *unconditioned stimulus*) was presented.

**D** Work with a partner. Summarize Pavlov's experiment by completing the following paragraph using terms from the reading:

Food (an _____ stimulus) naturally makes a dog salivate (an _____

response). If we always ring a bell (a _____ stimulus) as we feed the dog,

after a while, the dog will salivate when it hears the bell even without the food

(a _____ response).

## 2 Using telegraphic language Ⓝ Ⓛ Ⓢ

Lecture note taking is a complex skill, and developing it requires a great deal of practice, especially in a foreign language. One of the first things to learn about lecture note taking is that it is not possible to write down every word. More importantly, it is not a good idea! Many lecturers repeat themselves, go off the topic, and tell unrelated personal stories.

Good note takers can recognize what is important and what is not. They are able to get the important information down on paper in as few words as possible, using abbreviations and symbols. At the same time, they organize the information on the page to show what is a main point and what is a detail or example. These are all important skills to develop, and as you study this book, you will practice each of them.

The first step, however, is to learn to listen to several sentences of a lecture and quickly summarize the information in your own words. You must also train yourself to leave out unnecessary words, such as articles, prepositions, relative pronouns, the verb *be*, and other linking verbs. In other words, you need to learn to use what is called *telegraphic language*.

**A** Read the following telegraphic notes taken by a student listening to the lecture on stress and the immune system. Each of the four lines summarizes an important point in the lecture. With a partner, discuss what the abbreviated words mean.

☐ research* shows: imm. syst. hurt by stress (*animal & hum)

☐ headache, high bld. press. etc – more docs now treat w/relax. techniques (not drugs)

☐ headache, heart dis, high bld. press. etc (health probs) – may be part psych.

☐ med. profs: mind affects body – esp; neg. if feel 'helpless, no control.'

🔊 **B** Now watch or listen to the four short excerpts and match them with the correct
📹 telegraphic notes in Step A. Write the numbers in the boxes.

**C** Compare your choices with your partner and then as a class. Do you agree?

# 1 Breaking down words to guess their meaning

> When you see or hear an unknown word, try to guess at least part of its meaning by dividing it into parts that you recognize, as you did on page 12 with the word *psychosomatic.*

**A** Complete the definitions with word part meanings from the right column.

A word that contains:

| | |
|---|---|
| *psych-* is related to the _____ . | **1.** before |
| *-logy, -logic,* or *-logical* describes the _____ of a subject. | **2.** bad |
| *pre-* refers to something happening _____ . | **3.** study |
| *mal-* usually refers to something _____ . | **4.** mind or thinking |
| *phys-* has something to do with the _____ . | **5.** body |

**B** Compare answers as a class.

# 2 Guessing vocabulary from context

> Context plays two very important roles for the language learner. First, context can help us begin to understand the meaning of a completely new word. Second, context helps to widen our understanding of a word that we have already learned because words often have different meanings depending on how they are used.

**A** Work with a partner. Read the following phrases from Part 1 of the lecture. Some of the words in **bold** may be unfamiliar to you; try to guess their meaning based on the context. Your answers to the preceding exercise on parts of words should help you with some of these.

It seems **obvious** that the mind will have an effect on the body . . . and . . . in recent years we've gathered . . . some hard **data** that this is true . . .
. . . the way that you think actually affects the way that your body feels. . . . stress has real **implications** . . . for . . . in terms of what it can do to the body . . .
. . . psychosomatic disorders, . . . where there is a **physical** symptom caused by a **psychological** problem . . .
It's a real hot topic in psychology today . . . and **relevant** to almost all areas of our lives . . .
. . . the body's immune system inactivates foreign invaders and **removes** them from the body . . .
. . . a situation where there was uncontrollable or **unpredictable** stress, like electric shocks . . .
When rats were placed in an **environment** like that . . .

**B** Now match the **bold** words from Step A with the best definitions on the right:

| | |
|---|---|
| **1.** obvious | **a.** ___ to cause to go away; to get rid of |
| **2.** data | **b.** ___ easy to see or to realize |
| **3.** implications | **c.** ___ relating to the body |
| **4.** physical | **d.** ___ facts; information |
| **5.** psychological | **e.** ___ not able to be seen before it happens |
| **6.** relevant | **f.** ___ where we are; our surroundings |
| **7.** to remove | **g.** ___ relating to the mind |
| **8.** unpredictable | **h.** ___ important consequences or results |
| **9.** environment | **i.** ___ having importance; related |

**C** This exercise contains some more words from Part 1 of the lecture, shown in context. Use the context to help you choose the best definition for each word in **bold**.

**1.** We have some **hard** data to show that that is true.
   a. difficult     b. dependable     c. medical

**2.** . . . in **psychosomatic** disorders, a physical symptom is caused by a psychological problem.
   a. affecting the mind     b. caused by the mind     c. very dangerous

**3.** Headaches, . . . high blood pressure, . . . heart disease . . . all of these **symptoms** may be related to psychosomatic disorders.
   a. diseases     b. problems a doctor notices     c. problems a patient feels

**4.** . . . to recognize foreign **invaders**, things that come into the body . . .
   a. animals     b. attackers     c. medicines

**5.** The immune system is **compromised**, damaged, by certain stressors.
   a. improved     b. assisted     c. hurt

**6.** If we can condition immune systems to **malfunction**, then it makes sense that we could also condition them to get better.
   a. speed up     b. work harder     c. not work correctly

**D** Compare answers with a partner. Ask your teacher for help if you need to.

# 3 Summarizing what you have heard Ⓝ Ⓛ Ⓥ Ⓢ

Summarizing involves reducing a long piece of text (written or spoken) to a few clear sentences in your own words. With something as long as a lecture, summarizing is the last step. During the lecture, take notes in whatever way works best for you. After the lecture, go over your notes, reconstruct what you have heard, and decide which material is important. Now you are ready to write your summary. Summarizing is an essential skill because it shows that you have understood what is important in a reading or a lecture. It also provides you with a record that you can use to review the lecture content.

**A** The following is an incomplete summary of Part 1 of the lecture. Read the summary and think about what kinds of words or phrases might go in the blanks. Do not write anything yet.

### "Stress and the Immune System," Part 1

There is a lot of evidence to support the idea that our minds can affect our _____ . Many of the health problems that people suffer, such as headaches, _____ , and _____ , may be related to psychosomatic disorders – that is, they may be caused by the _____ . The field of psychoneuroimmunology (PNI) studies the way in which our minds can affect our _____ . In a healthy person, the immune system protects the body against _____ . Animal and human research has shown that stress – especially uncontrollable stress – can hurt the immune system. Robert Ader did an important study with rats in which he learned, quite by accident, that the rats' _____ could be conditioned to _____ . This was an exciting discovery for science: If the immune system can be taught to _____ , that probably means that it can also learn to _____ .

**B** Now watch or listen to Part 1 of the lecture. Take notes on your own paper. Remember, do not write down everything that you hear. Use the summary above as a guide to help you listen for the important points. Use telegraphic language in your notes to save time.

**C** Use your notes to complete the summary above. The words and phrases in the box below will help you. You will not need to use all of them. One of the terms is used twice.

| | | |
|---|---|---|
| bodies | disease | not work correctly |
| heal itself | heart disease | high blood pressure |
| illness | high cholesterol | immune systems |
| malfunction | mind | skin rashes |

**D** Compare summaries with a partner. Do you have similar answers? You do not need to have exactly the same words.

# 1 Learning words as they are used Ⓥ

> It's a good idea to learn words as they are used – not by themselves, but in phrases. That way you will be more likely to use them correctly yourself.

**A** Read the following excerpts from the lecture. The words in **bold** can have different meanings. Choose the meaning that best matches the way the word is used in the lecture excerpt.

**1.** . . . we know that people **under** . . . stress – when we analyze some of their immune functioning – [. . .] their immune systems become compromised.
The word *under* means:    a. in the process    b. not as much    c. who feel

**2.** So if you think in terms of **classical** conditioning, like Pavlov and his experiments with dogs . . .
The word *classical* means:
a. traditional    b. 18th–19th century    c. from ancient Greece

**3.** . . . the mental stress of just thinking about the exam . . . is acting as a conditioned stimulus to **depress** the immune system . . .
The word *depress* means:
a. cause to be less active    b. cause to be flat    c. cause to be sad

**4.** . . . today it is widely accepted in the medical **field** . . . uh . . . among health care professionals . . .
The word *field* means:
a. subject of study    b. profession    c. wide exterior space

**5.** . . . the mind has a powerful effect on the body, and . . . this effect is especially **negative** when a patient feels helpless . . .
The word *negative* means:
a. saying no    b. less than zero    c. unhealthful

**6.** . . . the mind can exert a **positive** influence on the body . . . in the case of problems like headaches. . . . Um, more and more health care providers are teaching patients to control these by simple relaxation techniques.
The word *positive* means:
a. with no doubt    b. healthful    c. cheerful

**B** Compare your choices with a partner and then as a class.

# 2 Guessing vocabulary from context Ⓥ Ⓝ Ⓢ

**A** Read the following excerpts from Part 2 of the lecture. Then use your own words to complete the definitions of the words in **bold**.

**1.** . . . when people are under great stress, for example, **accountants** before tax time . . .
Accountants are professionals who figure people's _____ .

**2.** . . . elderly people in **nursing homes** . . .
Nursing homes are residences for _____ .

**3.** . . . the ones who felt in control **tended to** be healthier . . .

A person who **tends to** be healthier than other people is _____ healthier.

**4. Relaxation techniques** can be very effective . . . more effective than **medication**.

An example of a relaxation technique is _____ .

_____ is a very common medication.

**B** Compare what you wrote with a partner. Do you agree? Your answers do not have to be the same. Ask your teacher for help if necessary.

## 3 Summarizing what you have heard Ⓝ Ⓛ Ⓢ

**A** Read the following incomplete summary of Part 2 of the lecture. Be sure that you understand all the words. Think about what information you will need to fill in the blanks.

### "Stress and the Immune System," Part 2

There are also _____ studies to support the idea that the mind can

_____ . Simply thinking about stressful situations can _____ the

immune system. This has been seen in studies on accountants before tax time, and

on _____ before _____ . Also, if people feel out of _____

in their lives, this can compromise their _____ . Studies show that people

in nursing homes who didn't choose to _____ are more likely to get sick

than people who _____ . People in the _____ field are becoming

more interested in PNI. We see this, for example, in the treatment of headaches and

_____ ; more doctors and nurses today are teaching their _____

to control these problems not with medication, but rather with _____ .

**B** Now watch or listen to Part 2 of the lecture. Take notes on your own paper. Remember to use telegraphic language.

**C** Use your notes to complete the summary above. Choose from the words and phrases in the box if you need to supplement your notes. You will not need to use all of them.

| | | |
|---|---|---|
| affect the body | control | depress |
| did (= chose to live there) | disease | exams |
| human | get better | patients |
| heal itself | high blood pressure | immune systems |
| sleeplessness | influence the body | live there |
| medical | students | relaxation techniques |

**D** Compare summaries with a partner. Remember, your summaries do not have to be identical.

# 1 Comparing information from different sources

The following is from the U.C. Berkeley *Wellness Newsletter*. Read it and discuss the questions as a class.

**Various studies on stress and immunology found that:**

- During times of great stress – for example, exams – students' immune cells became less active, and their resistance to disease decreased.

- "Highly stressed" people caught colds more easily than other people.

- People who had recently lost a husband or wife had higher rates of illness and death than others.

- Patients with cancer lived longer if they had a "fighting spirit," and cancer patients who felt depressed about their illness died sooner.

1. Is this information consistent with what Professor Cash described?

2. Do you have any personal experience that supports these findings? For example, have you (or someone you know) ever gotten sick during a stressful time?

# 2 Sharing your cultural perspective ⓢ

An issue becomes more interesting if you share your own cultural perspective on it and hear the perspective of people from other cultures.

## Discuss the following questions in a small group:

1. As Professor Cash stated in her lecture, Western culture has come to view chronic stress as a serious problem that can ultimately damage our health, and the medical field has begun to acknowledge that many physical disorders (skin rashes, high blood pressure, headaches, etc.) may in fact be linked to mental stress. What are the most common physical problems that people in your culture complain about? Headaches? Fatigue? Are they the same for men and women? Do they differ depending on age? Compare notes in your group.

2. Now think about how people traditionally view these common problems in your culture. Do they see them as only physical? Do they take medication? Go to the doctor? Or do people see these problems as something they can treat themselves, without medication?

# Chapter 2
# Lifestyle and Health

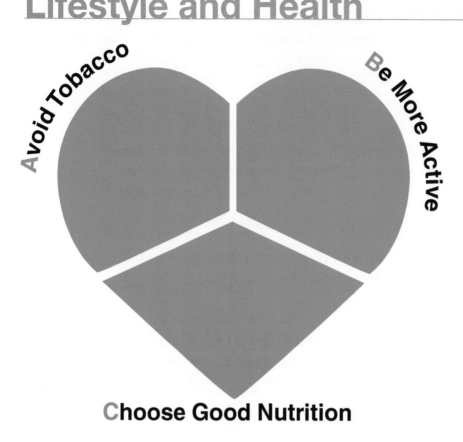

Choose Good Nutrition

Look at the image above and answer the questions with a partner.

1. Given the title of this chapter, what do you think this graphic represents?
2. Read the three phrases written around it. What do they mean?

## 1 Getting Started

In this section, you are going to discuss what people can do to get healthy or stay healthy, and you will perform a small experiment involving your muscles and heart rate.

# 1 Reading and thinking about the topic Ⓥ Ⓢ

**A** Read the following passage taken from the Mayo Clinic Web site. As a class, check your understanding of the five strategies by restating them in your own words.

### Five medication-free strategies to help prevent heart disease

You can prevent heart disease by following a heart-healthy lifestyle. Here are five strategies to help you protect your heart:

1. Don't smoke or use tobacco products.
2. Get active.
3. Eat a heart-healthy diet.
4. Maintain a healthy weight.
5. Get regular health screenings.

**B** Answer the following questions:

1. What are the five recommended strategies supposed to help you do?
2. Compare the three recommendations included in the graphic (on previous page) with the five in the reading. How are they different?
3. Is this reading addressed to people who have heart disease? Support your answer.

**C** Discuss your own experiences and opinions with a partner.

1. Do you have a "heart-healthy lifestyle"? Review the five guidelines in the reading. Do you follow them? Which ones are most important for you?
2. Do you know any people who have had heart problems? If so, do you think that their lifestyle could be a contributing factor?
3. The title implies that a "medication-free" strategy is better than one that involves drugs. Do you agree?

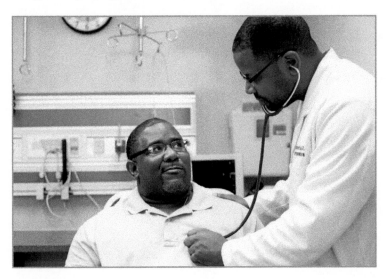

## 2 Recalling what you already know Ⓢ

> Recalling what you already know about a topic beforehand will make a discussion of that topic easier for you to follow.

Take turns asking and answering the following questions with a partner. Make your answers as clear and as simple as you can.

1. What does the term *heart rate* mean?
2. How can you measure your heart rate?
3. What happens when your heart beats?
4. Your heart rate does not stay the same all the time. How and why does it change?

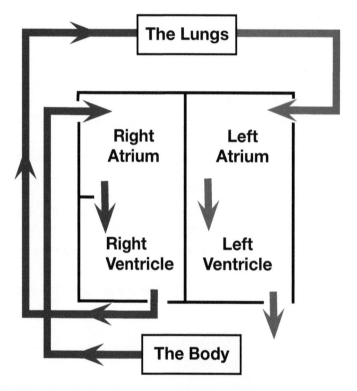

How the human heart works

# 3 Following directions L S

🔊 **A** Listen to the audio and follow the speaker's directions.

| Your Results | | |
|---|---|---|
| 1st heart rate: ___ | 2nd heart rate: ___ | Rate increase: ___ |

**B** Discuss the following questions in a small group:

1. Were your heart rates faster the second time that you measured them? If so, explain why as clearly and as completely as you can.
2. What are some other activities, situations, or conditions that can cause heart rate to increase?
3. In general, which indicates a healthier heart when you are at rest: a fast or a slow rate?

**C** Figure out the class averages for the heart rates and the average increase. Record them.

| Class Results | | |
|---|---|---|
| 1st average: ___ | 2nd average: ___ | Average increase: ___ |

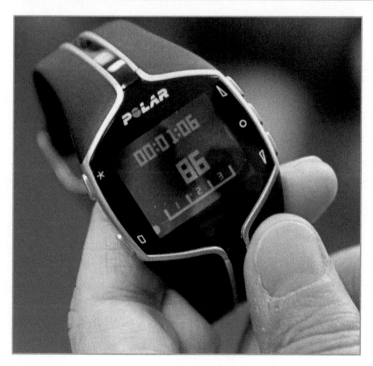

# 2 Real-Life Voices

In this section, you will hear interviews with Pat and Donna, two people who used to smoke.

## BEFORE THE INTERVIEWS

## Predicting the content Ⓢ

**A** Answer the following questions with a partner based on your own opinions and experience:

1. Why do people start smoking?
2. Why is it so difficult to quit smoking?
3. What are some of the methods that people use to stop smoking?
4. What are some of the benefits of giving up smoking?

**B** Share answers as a class.

Teens often start smoking because of peer pressure.

## INTERVIEW 1  Starting Smoking and Trying to Quit

## 1 Examining vocabulary in context Ⓥ

Here are some words and expressions from the interview with Pat, printed in **bold** and given in the context in which you will hear them. They are followed by definitions.

I smoked **heavily**: *a lot; a great deal*

Smoking was **cool**: *good; socially desirable* [informal]

**peer pressure**: *feeling the need to do something because one's friends are doing it*

It never **did any good**: *had no effect; was not helpful*

**just [used] will power**: *made a decision to do something difficult and tried to keep doing it*

I wasn't **hooked** anymore: *addicted (as to a drug)* [informal]

You've never been **tempted** to start smoking again?: *wanted to do something badly but haven't actually done it*

## 2 Anticipating answers Ⓛ Ⓝ Ⓢ

When you listen to an interview, you can improve your comprehension by focusing on the interviewer's questions. For example, if the interviewer begins a question with "**How long** have you . . .?" what do you expect that the answer will be? It will probably be a **number of months or years**. Anticipating what you will hear improves your ability to understand it when you do hear it.

**A** You will hear the interviewer ask Pat the following questions. First, read the questions; for each question, guess what kind of answer Pat will give.

1. Pat, **when** did you **start** [smoking]?
2. And **how long** did you **smoke**?
3. **Why** did you **start** smoking in the first place?
4. **How much** did you **smoke**? **How many cigarettes** a day?
5. **What method** did you use to **try to quit**?
6. **How** did you finally **quit**?
7. So you**'ve never** been tempted to start smoking again?
8. **How** did quitting **affect** your health?
9. **What advice** would you **give** to someone who's trying to quit smoking?

**B** Now read Pat's incomplete answers below. Then listen to the interview and complete Pat's answers.

1. I was probably . . . ___ , ___ .
2. ___ years on cigarettes and then a pipe for about ___ years.
3. It was _____ .
4. At the peak, a _____ .
5. Just _____ .
6. I had a _____ and I couldn't smoke in the _____ .
7. ___ ! In fact, I dream about it every once in a while, and it's more like a nightmare.
8. I had a lot more _____ , my _____ got easier. . . . All kinds of things – uh . . . walking, _____ , . . . singing, _____ . . . . My son and I were doing a lot of backpacking at that time, and that got a lot _____ after I _____ .
9. Have a _____? Mmm . . . seriously, I really _____ give advice.

**C** Now compare your answers in Step B with a partner. Use the words or phrases in the box below to check your answers. Listen again if you need to.

| 5 | 13 | 14 | 20 |
|---|---|---|---|
| biking | breathing | cool | easier |
| energy | heart attack | hospital | no |
| pack and a half | stopped smoking | running | will power |
| wouldn't | | | |

# 1 Examining vocabulary in context Ⓥ

Here are some words and expressions used in Part 1 of the interview with Donna printed in **bold** and given in the context in which you will hear them. They are followed by definitions.

Smoking is a social habit.

A lot of my friends **would** get together after school: *did as a habit; used to*

I **went up to about** a pack a day: *increased the number of cigarettes*

in South America as **an exchange student**: *one who attends school for a while in another country, living with a family*

I started getting **bronchitis**: *inflammation of the airways leading to the lungs*

I had **chronic** bronchitis: *occurring repeatedly or lasting for a long time*

**initially**: *at first*

I just **went cold turkey**: *stopped using a drug suddenly and completely*

I experienced **withdrawal**: *symptoms that appear when you stop taking an addictive drug*

# 2 Paraphrasing what you have heard Ⓝ Ⓛ Ⓢ

As a student, you will often need to restate information that you have heard or read. This task requires you to grasp the message completely enough to paraphrase it – that is, to express the same ideas with different words. When you paraphrase, you are showing not only that you remember what you heard or read, but also that you understand it.

**A** Read the incomplete paraphrase of Part 1 of the interview with Donna. It is divided into three sections. Think about what kind of information you will need to complete each section.

**How She Started** – Donna started smoking at about age _____ or _____ .

She and her friends would get together after _____ . They would eat _____

and smoke cigarettes. Donna's _____ didn't know about it.

**Addicted to Cigarettes** – After a while, Donna was smoking a _____ a day.

She kept smoking for _____ more years. Donna studied in South _____ and

later she taught in _____ . In both places, smoking was more _____ than

in the United States. People smoked in public places – for example, in _____ ,

_____ , and _____ .

**Trying to Quit** – But Donna wasn't feeling very _____ . She had chronic

bronchitis. She tried to _____ smoking many times but could not. Later, when

she was married and _____ , she almost completely stopped smoking. But it

was very _____ for her, and as soon as her _____ was born, she

started _____ again.

🔊 **B** Now listen to Part 1 of the interview with Donna. Complete the paraphrase in Step A by filling in the blanks as you listen. Refer to the words and phrases in the box below if you need to. Note that some of the words in the box are examples that Donna gives in the interview; you will not need all of them to complete the paraphrase.

| | | | |
|---|---|---|---|
| 13 | 16 | 17 | America |
| buses | candy | classrooms | common |
| Mexico | movie | pack | painful |
| parents | pregnant | quit | school |
| smoking | son | theaters | supermarkets |
| taxicabs | well | | |

**C** Compare answers as a class. Listen again if you need to.

# 1 Examining vocabulary in context Ⓥ

Here are some words and expressions used in Part 2 of the interview with Donna printed in **bold** and given in the context in which you will hear them. They are followed by definitions.

**social pressure** to quit [smoking]: *other people trying to influence how we act, trying to make us act differently (e.g., quit smoking), often by expressing disapproval*

People would really **react negatively**: *be upset; show disapproval*

This woman **hypnotized** him: *put someone into a sleeplike state, then gave him or her suggestions*

I had four **treatments**: *appointments with someone who gives a service (e.g., a hypnotherapist)*

completely lost the **urge** to smoke: *desire; temptation*

This was **like** five years ago: *approximately; I'm guessing* [slang; very common in speech]

completely **fed up with it** [e.g., smoking]: *tired of something; not wanting to do it anymore*

I would **do everything in my power** to educate him: *do all that I can; make my strongest effort*

the health **hazards** of smoking: *dangers*

My **lung function** improved: *ability to breathe*

I started exercising . . . so that improved my **metabolism**: *how the body converts food into energy*

celebrate our **anniversary**: *the date every year on which something important happened*

## 2 Paraphrasing what you have heard Ⓝ Ⓛ Ⓢ

**A** Read the incomplete paraphrase of Part 2 of the interview with Donna. It is divided into four sections. As you read, think about what kind of information you will need to fill in the blanks.

**Social Pressure** – Donna's friends and even her _____ really pressured her to stop smoking, especially when she was around their _____ .

**Hypnotherapy** – Finally, a friend of Donna's recommended a hypnotherapist. This friend had been a very heavy smoker – __ packs a _____ – but the hypnotherapist had helped him _____ and the treatment was _____ . Donna decided to go and try it herself, and the treatment _____ ! Donna believes that she was successful this time for two reasons: (1) Hypnotherapy was the right _____ for her; and (2) she was finally _____ with smoking and _____ to quit.

**Donna's Son and Smoking** – Donna does not think that her son will ever _____ smoking because he _____ it when she smoked. He worried about her _____ . However, if he *did* start smoking, she would do everything she could to _____ him about the health _____ of smoking before he became _____ to cigarettes.

**The Benefits of Quitting** – As soon as she quit smoking, Donna started to feel _____ physically; she had more _____ , and she could _____ things again. Also, food started to _____ to her. She started _____ to control her weight. A final advantage was saving _____ .

🔊 **B** Now listen to Part 2 of the interview with Donna. Complete the paraphrase in Step A as you listen. Refer to the words and phrases in the box below if you need to.

| | | | |
|---|---|---|---|
| **3** | **addicted** | **better** | **dangers** |
| **day** | **educate** | **energy** | **exercising** |
| **fed up** | **hated** | **health** | **kids** |
| **method** | **money** | **painless** | **quit** |
| **ready** | **sister** | **smell** | **start** |
| **taste better** | **worked** | | |

**C** Compare answers as a class. Listen again if you need to.

## 3 Drawing inferences 🄛 🄢

🔊 **A** Read the incomplete statements below, then listen to the interview excerpts and make inferences based on what you hear. Circle the correct letter to complete the statements.

1. Pat probably ___ his high school basketball coach.
   a. was afraid of
   b. disliked
   c. respected

2. Pat is probably ___ about the 30 pounds that he gained.
   a. upset
   b. not very concerned
   c. happy

3. Donna ___ that her son will grow up to be a smoker.
   a. doesn't believe
   b. worries
   c. is sure

4. Donna probably cut back on smoking when she got pregnant because she was ___ .
   a. having trouble with bronchitis
   b. concerned for her baby's health
   c. finally ready to stop

**B** Compare your answers with a partner.

### AFTER THE INTERVIEWS

# Combining information from different sources 🄢 🄝

An important academic skill is taking information from different sources and *synthesizing* it – that is, combining it to create something new, such as a generalization. The first step in synthesizing is to collect the information in one place.

**A** Complete the accompanying chart. Under Pat and Donna, write an X for all the answers that you heard in the interviews. Write a "?" if you are not sure that Pat or Donna specifically stated one of the answers, but you infer that it is true.

| | | Pat | Donna |
|---|---|---|---|
| **Why did you start smoking?** | Peer pressure | | |
| | It was "cool." | | |
| | Cigarette advertising | | |
| **What physical problems did smoking cause?** | Heart disease | | |
| | Bronchitis | | |
| | Low energy | | |
| | Inability to taste and smell | | |
| **What methods(s) did you use to try to quit?** | Will power | | |
| | Candy | | |
| | Hypnosis | | |
| **Do you ever feel like smoking now?** | Yes | | |
| | No | | |
| **What advice would you give to people trying to quit smoking?** | Talk to them about the health dangers | | |
| | No advice | | |
| **In what ways is your life better now?** | Enjoy taste of food more | | |
| | More physically active | | |
| | Easier to breathe | | |
| | More energy | | |
| | Save money | | |
| **What physical activities do you enjoy?** | Backpacking | | |
| | Biking | | |
| | Running | | |

**B** Compare charts with a partner. Discuss and explain your answers. Your guesses may not be exactly the same.

# 3 In Your Own Voice

In this section, you will discuss and conduct research on smoking and other habits that affect your health.

Answer the questions below:

1. Do you smoke now? _____ If yes, have you ever tried to quit? _____
2. If no, have you ever been a smoker? _____
3. Do you have friends or family members who smoke now? _____ If yes, has that person ever tried to quit? _____
4. Do you have friends or family members who have quit smoking? _____

## Asking for confirmation Ⓢ Ⓛ Ⓝ

> Asking for confirmation is a very important skill in a foreign language. When someone tells you something and you want to be sure that you understood her correctly, repeat the key words that you heard or paraphrase them, and use question intonation (rising voice). This tactic has an added advantage: It slows down the conversation a little so that you can follow it more easily.

🔊 **A** You are going to share your answers in Step A with another student. But first, listen to how the interviewer asks Pat for confirmation as she is interviewing him about smoking. Pay attention to her intonation.

> **Expressions used by the interviewer to ask for confirmation of what she heard**
>
> I understand that you used to smoke. Is that correct?
> So, now, you started smoking when you were about 13, and you smoked for 25 years, did you say?
> Back to the cigarettes, huh?
> A heart attack!?
> Do you mean you've never been tempted to start smoking again?

**B** Work with a partner. Look at his/her answers to the questions in Step A and choose one question to be the topic of your interview. Make your own interview questions or use the questions from the chart in *AFTER THE INTERVIEWS* on page 31. Let your partner speak freely, and use the expressions above and those in the box below to confirm that you heard him/her correctly. For example:

_____ , *I understand that your father smokes. Is that right?*
*Did you say that you started smoking when you were 16?*

**C** Make brief notes as your partner answers your questions. If you have time, interview a second classmate on a different question from Step A.

---

### Some additional ways to ask for confirmation

Excuse me, do you mean that . . .?
Did you say that you . . .?
In other words, he finally quit smoking when . . .?
So you're saying that . . .?

---

**D** As a class, share what you learned about your classmates.

# 4 Academic Listening and Note Taking

In this section, you will hear and take notes on a two-part lecture given by Kristine Moore, a registered nurse and clinical nursing specialist. The title of the lecture is "Risk Factors in Cardiovascular Disease." Ms. Moore will discuss what conditions and habits make a person more likely to have cardiovascular problems.

## 1 Building background knowledge on the topic

> If the title of a lecture has a technical term in it, look it up beforehand in a good English–English dictionary. If the definition contains other terms you are not familiar with, look these up as well. The dictionary entries for these other terms may lead you to look up still more new words. The new vocabulary that you learn in this way will help you to understand the lecture better.

**A** The lecture that you will hear deals with cardiovascular disease. To get a better understanding of what cardiovascular disease is, read the dictionary entries below.

> **artery** *(noun, Anatomy)* Any of a branching system of tubular vessels that carry blood away from the heart
> **blood vessel** *(noun)* An elastic canal shaped like a tube that carries blood to or from the heart, such as an artery or a vein
> **cardio-** *(prefix)* Relating to the heart
> **cardiovascular** *(adjective)* Involving, or relating to, the heart and the blood vessels
> **vein** *(noun, Anatomy)* Any of a branching system of tubular vessels that carry blood toward the heart

**B** Answer the following questions with a partner:

1. What do you think *vascular* means?
2. What is the difference between an artery and a vein?
3. What word in the definitions means "tube?"

## 2 Predicting the content

> Sometimes you can predict a great deal from the title of a lecture. Doing this will usually increase your listening comprehension.

**A** Discuss the following questions in a small group:

1. The lecture title is "Risk Factors in Cardiovascular Disease." What are some serious health problems that affect the cardiovascular system?
2. What risk factors do you think the lecturer will present? Try to name some habits or conditions that can increase a person's risk for cardiovascular disease.

**B** As a class, compile your predictions on the board.

# 3 Using symbols and abbreviations Ⓝ Ⓛ Ⓢ

When you take notes during a lecture, you have to write down a lot of information very quickly. Rather than writing every word in full, develop the habit of using *symbols* and *abbreviations*. Some common examples of each are given here in **bold** with their meanings in parentheses ( ).

*Symbols* Here are some symbols commonly used in English. Many of them come from mathematics.

**&** (and)
**=** (the same as, means)
**@** (at)
**≠** (different from, doesn't mean)
**<** (less than)
**∴** (therefore)
**>** (greater than)

*Abbreviations* Good note takers also commonly abbreviate (shorten) long or frequently occurring words. Some abbreviations are standard: Any English speaker will know what they mean. Here are some standard abbreviations. Notice that some are based on Latin words.

**abt.** (about)
**e.g.** (for example, from the Latin *exempli gratia*)
**gov't** (government)
**A.M.** (before noon, from the Latin *ante meridiem*)
**hosp.** (hospital)
**P.M.** (after noon, from the Latin *post meridiem*)
**MD** (medical doctor)
**intell.** (intelligence, intelligent)
**med.** (medicine, medical)
**IQ** (intelligence quotient)
**TV** (television)
**admin.** (administration, administrative)
**w/** (with)
**b/c** (because)

You may want to adopt some of these symbols and abbreviations, and you will probably also want to invent some of your own, depending on the content of the lecture you are hearing. When you invent symbols and abbreviations, it is important to review your notes as soon as possible after the lecture, while their meanings are still fresh in your mind.

**A** Study the symbols and abbreviations on the left. Match them with their meanings on the right. Notice the way in which each of the abbreviations was created.

___ **1.** CVD    **a.** is; means; is the same as

___ **2.** PVD    **b.** with

___ **3.** →    **c.** artery; arteries

___ **4.** e.g.    **d.** reduce; lower; decrease

___ **5.** ↑    **e.** increase; higher

___ **6.** ↓    **f.** high blood pressure

___ **7.** pers.    **g.** at least; greater than or equal to

___ **8.** HBP    **h.** female; women

___ **9.** =    **i.** male; men

___ **10.** art.    **j.** causes; results in

___ **11.** ♀    **k.** for example

___ **12.** ♂    **l.** peripheral vascular disease

___ **13.** ♥    **m.** cardiovascular disease

___ **14.** w/    **n.** heart

___ **15.** ≥    **o.** person; personality

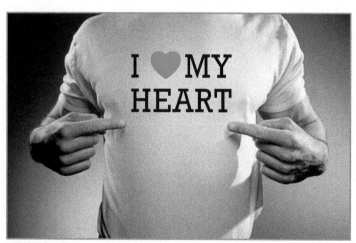

**B** Compare your answers with a partner.

 **C** Now watch or listen to four excerpts from the lecture. Take notes on your own paper as you listen, using symbols and abbreviations. The ones mentioned above are only suggestions; you may use different ones if you prefer. Remember also to leave out unimportant words, as you did in the task *Using telegraphic language*, in Chapter 1, page 13.

**D** Use your notes to tell a partner what you heard. Did you hear the same things?

# 1 Guessing vocabulary from context Ⓥ

**A** The items below contain some important vocabulary from Part 1 of the lecture. Each of the terms is shown in **bold**, in the context in which you will hear it. Work with a partner. Take turns explaining what you think each term means, based on its context. In some cases, you may be able to give only a general idea, but this can still contribute to your overall understanding of the term. For example, is it a noun or an adjective? Does it mean something good or something bad?

___ 1. . . . a loss of **elasticity**, so the arteries aren't as flexible . . .

___ 2. . . . **partial** or complete blocking of the arteries . . .

___ 3. In a **stroke**, there is blocking of the arteries that feed the brain.

___ 4. . . . **peripheral** vascular disease, which is also known as clots to the legs . . .

___ 5. In **clots** to the legs, there is blockage of one or more arteries.

___ 6. . . . **estrogen**, a hormone which is made in women's bodies . . .

___ 7. . . . a hormone which is made in women's bodies up until **menopause** . . .

___ 8. People with **diabetes** have a higher rate of cardiovascular disease.

___ 9. . . . certain amounts of fats that our bodies use **metabolically** . . .

___ 10. . . . **cholesterol**, and some of these other fat-containing chemicals . . .

___ 11. And this is to some extent **hereditary** . . . usually it's because of family history.

**B** Match each vocabulary term in Step A with its definition below. Write the letter. Note that the definitions reflect the context in which the terms are used in the lecture; some of these terms can have different meanings in other contexts.

**a.** not complete; in part

**b.** a chemical produced in females

**c.** acting as fuel to make the body work

**d.** wax-like material produced by the body and necessary for its functioning

**e.** the time of life after which women can no longer have children

**f.** inherited; passed from one generation to the next

**g.** flexibility; ability to bend and stretch

**h.** balls of fat that block blood flow in arteries

**i.** disease in which the body cannot make insulin, which controls blood sugar

**j.** happening away from the center of the body

**k.** breaking or blocking of a blood vessel in the brain, often resulting in the loss of some bodily functions

## 2 Outlining practice Ⓝ Ⓛ Ⓢ

> An outline gives you a visual picture of the organization of a lecture or reading. In a formal outline, main points are designated as I, II, III, and so forth. Under each main point, there are usually supporting points designated as A, B, C, and so on. Creating an outline from your notes is a good way to review the material and to show that you understand the relationships between main and supporting points.

**A** Look at the following incomplete outline of Part 1 of the lecture. It shows the main and supporting points you will hear. Study the outline; think about what kind of information you will need in order to complete it.

| "Risk Factors in Cardiovascular Disease," Part 1 |
| --- |
| I.  CVD = heart attack, stroke, peripheral vascular disease<br>    A. ♥ attack = _____<br>    B. _____ = _____<br>    C. PVD = _____<br>II. Unalterable risk factors<br>    A. Gender: age <50, ♀ _____<br>    B. Age: older = _____<br>    _____ |

**B** Now watch or listen to Part 1 of the lecture. Take notes on your own paper. Remember to use symbols and abbreviations as much as possible.

**C** Use your notes to complete the outline. You do not need to include everything that you heard; just fill in the blanks.

**D** Compare outlines with a partner. Did you record the same information?

**LECTURE PART 2**  Alterable Risk Factors in CVD

## 1 Guessing vocabulary from context Ⓥ Ⓢ

**A** The following items contain some important vocabulary from Part 2 of the lecture. With a partner, take turns explaining what you think each bold term means, based on its context. Even if you can't define a term completely, say as much as you can about it.

___ **1.** There are good medications that have very few **side effects**.

___ **2.** . . . often occurs in people who are **obese** – very overweight . . .

___ **3.** It's very important to get rid of that **excess** weight.

___ **4.** People who smoke cigarettes have a higher **incidence** of these diseases.

___ **5.** Tobacco use probably affects the way fats are **metabolized**.

___ **6.** . . . psychosocial factors, and this would include social **isolation** . . .

___ **7.** **Acute** stress results in higher blood pressure.

___ **8.** **Sedentary** lifestyle is the last factor to be added to the list.

**B** Match each vocabulary term in Step A with its definition below. Write the letter. Note that some of these terms can have different meanings in other contexts.

**a.** used as fuel for the body

**b.** very fat

**c.** very strong, very bad

**d.** extra; more than needed

**e.** being alone, separated from other people

**f.** not getting any physical exercise; sitting a lot

**g.** frequency; how often something happens

**h.** unwanted results of taking a medication

# 2 Outlining practice Ⓝ Ⓛ Ⓢ

**A** Look at the following incomplete outline of Part 2 of the lecture. Study the outline; think about what kind of information you will need to complete it.

| "Risk Factors in Cardiovascular Disease," Part 2 |
|---|
| III. _____ |
|     **A.** HBP – Controlled w/ _____ |
|     **B.** _____ (≥20% _____) may → _____ and _____ |
|     **C.** _____ → _____ _____ and _____ |
|     **D.** Psychosoc. (= _____) may → _____ → CVD |
|     **E.** _____ |

**B** Now watch or listen to Part 2 of the lecture. Take notes on your own paper. Remember to use symbols and abbreviations as much as possible.

**C** Use your notes to complete the outline. Then compare outlines with a partner.

---

**AFTER THE LECTURE**

## Sharing your cultural perspective Ⓢ

**Discuss the following questions in a small group:**

1. Is there a high incidence of cardiovascular disease in your country? If yes, which of the risk factors mentioned in the lecture do you think are most responsible? If not, why not, in your opinion?

2. A recent study by the World Health Organization reported that 10 percent of smoking deaths worldwide every year are the result of "second-hand smoke" – that is, the people who died were not smokers, but they lived or worked with smokers. Is smoking controlled or prohibited in restaurants or other public places in your country? Do you think it should be?

# Unit 1 Academic Vocabulary Review

This section reviews the vocabulary from Chapters 1 and 2. Some of the words that you needed to learn to understand the content of this unit are specific to the topics of health and illness – what we might call *technical terms*. Other words belong to the standard Academic Word List used worldwide: They appear across different academic fields and are extremely useful for all students to know. We will call these terms *general academic vocabulary*. They are the focus of this review. For a complete list of all the Academic Word List words in this book, see the Appendix on pages 181–182.

## 1 Word forms

Read the sentences and fill in the blanks with a form of the word. For verbs, use the correct tense and person. For nouns, use the correct number (singular or plural). Note: You will not use all of the word forms given.

1. **to analyze, analysis, analytic:**
   The research group performed an _____ of immune functioning in rats.
   The research group _____ the rats' responses to different stimuli.

2. **to depress, depressive, depression:**
   Stress appears to have a _____ effect on the immune system.
   Stress can _____ the immune system.

3. **environment, environmental, environmentally:**
   One's physical _____ plays an important role in health.
   Two examples of _____ stressors are loud noise and bright lights.

4. **medical, medicine, medication, to medicate:**
   People with high blood pressure benefit from taking a combination of _____ .
   Obesity is a serious _____ problem.
   Doctors are trained to practice _____ .

5. **relevant, relevance:**
   The issue of stress-induced illness has _____ for all of us.
   Psychoneuroimmunology is _____ particularly to people under great stress.

6. **unpredictable, unpredictability, predictable, predictability, to predict:**
   When stress is _____ , it causes damage to the immune system.
   When we cannot _____ when something bad will happen, our systems are more likely to be hurt by stress.
   The _____ of stress increases its negative effects.
   _____ stress is less of a problem for the immune system.

7. **complex, complexity:**
   The _____ of obesity makes it very difficult to treat.

8. **isolation, to isolate, isolated:**
   A person who is socially _____ may be at greater risk for certain health problems.
   Social _____ may contribute indirectly to cardiovascular disease.

**9. occurrence, to occur:**

High blood pressure often _____ in very overweight people.

Stroke is a very rare _____ in people in their thirties.

**10. statistics, statistical, statistically, statistician:**

_____ show that people who smoke are more likely to get heart disease.

The difference in heart attack rates for smokers and nonsmokers is _____ significant.

# 2 Topic review

Read the questions. Each question is followed by a box containing related words and phrases from the unit. General academic vocabulary is given in **bold**. Answer the questions with a partner; the words and phrases in the boxes will help you to recall the answers.

## Stress and health

**1.** What are some of the causes of **stress**?

> **stressful job / assignment / environment / unpredictable /accountants / disruptive** children

**2.** What is the relationship between **stress** and illness?

> **energy / physical /** fatigue **/ compromised immune system / malfunction /** susceptible **/ research / documented**

**3.** How does our mental attitude affect our health?

> **obvious / energy / physical / compromised immune system / malfunction /** susceptible **/ psychological / psychosomatic / negative** attitude **/ relaxation** techniques / medication

## Risk factors in cardiovascular disease

**4.** Discuss the relationship between cardiovascular disease and the following risk **factors**: age, gender, diabetes, tobacco, weight, family history, lack of exercise.

> **alterable / unalterable / obvious /** obesity / cholesterol / greater **incidence /** metabolism / hereditary **/ function / implications / complex** disease **process / appropriate** medication

**5.** Discuss the possible relationship between cardiovascular disease and the mind.

> **isolation / psychosocial factors / depression /** acute **stress /** chronic **stress /** high-pressure **job / research / react / linked**

# Oral Presentation

As students, you will most likely be required to give oral presentations in English. In this section, you will be asked to conduct some research and present your results to the class.

## BEFORE THE PRESENTATION

## 1 Conducting a survey

**A** Think of a topic related to health or health habits, such as exercise, smoking, or dietary habits, or attitudes toward smoking, exercise, or diet. Keep the topic narrow so that your questions will give meaningful results.

**B** Write three or four questions about your topic. Write them in a multiple-choice format so that the responses will be easy to analyze. Here is an example:

> ### How many hours a week do you exercise?
> A. 0–1     B. 2–5     C. 6–10     D. >10

If a person answered, "I exercise about an hour a day," you would record the answer as C.

**C** Make a checklist like this one to record your answers. Survey at least 20 people.

| Students | Gender (M/F) | Nationality | Question 1 | | | | Question 2 | | | |
|---|---|---|---|---|---|---|---|---|---|---|
| | | | A | B | C | D | A | B | C | D |
| 1 | | Japanese | | | | | | | | |
| 2 | | Polish | | | | | | | | |
| 3 | | Mexican | | | | | | | | |
| etc. | | | | | | | | | | |

**D** Finally, analyze your data. Add up your responses. Compare answers by gender and by nationality. Are there any major differences between groups? Express the results in percentages and make notes to present a brief report for your class. For example:

> ♂s smoke >♀s – 60%♂ vs. 25% ♀

## 2 Using specific examples to support generalizations

A good oral presentation must be a balance of general and specific. General statements will get your audience's attention; examples will help them to understand and remember the generalizations. Examples generally follow a general statement, but they can also come first.

As you prepare and practice your presentation, include general statements about what you have learned and support them with examples from your research.

## 3 Providing visual support for a presentation

When you are presenting research results, think about how you can visually communicate what you have learned to your classmates. Numbers, for example, can be represented very effectively in a pie chart or a graph. Make copies for your class or use the board.

## Keys to a successful presentation: Eye contact and pacing

**Eye contact.** It is very important to look at your audience when you speak; they will hear you much better and be more interested in what you have to say. Practice in front of a mirror until you feel comfortable looking directly at yourself in the mirror as you speak.

**Pacing.** It is natural to feel a bit nervous when giving a speech, and we have a tendency to speak more quickly when we feel nervous. But remember, your classmates are listening to a foreign language. You can help increase their listening comprehension by speaking slowly and pausing briefly between sections of your presentation. If you feel nervous, stop and take a deep breath.

When it is your turn to give your presentation, hand out copies of your graph or post a large copy in front of the classroom. Speak slowly and loudly. Refer to your graph to help your classmates understand the points you are making. Look at your classmates as you speak. You may look down at your notes, but then look up again – do not read your presentation. And have fun!

## Inviting and responding to audience questions

When you give a presentation, plan to allow at least five minutes at the end for audience questions. You can greatly improve your classmates' understanding of your talk if you are willing to go over any points they may have missed. Remember, you are the expert.

When you finish your presentation, ask your classmates if they have any questions. Here is some language that you can use.

| Asking for Questions/Comments | Responding to Questions |
|---|---|
| *Does anyone have a question?* <br> *May I answer any questions?* <br> *Is there anything that was unclear to you?* <br> *Do you have any questions or comments about the graph?* <br> *Are there any other questions or comments?* | *That's a good question. What I meant was . . .* <br> *Yes, you're right, that is what I learned.* <br> *No, actually, what I meant was . . .* <br> *If you look at this part of the graph, it shows . . .* <br> *Thank you for your comment.* |

# Unit 2
# Development Through Life

In this unit, you will hear people discuss two stages of human development. Chapter 3 deals with the teen years. You will hear two teenagers talk about their lives, and then hear a lecture on the transition from the teens to adulthood. Chapter 4 addresses adulthood. You will hear people of all ages talk about the challenges and joys of being adults, and then hear a lecture on how early adulthood is changing in American culture.

# Contents

In Unit 2, you will listen to and speak about the following topics.

| Chapter 3<br>The Teen Years | Chapter 4<br>Adulthood |
|---|---|
| **Interview 1**<br>Being a Teenager in a Different Culture<br>**Interview 2**<br>Starting a New Life in One's Teens<br>**Lecture**<br>Erik Erikson's Fifth Stage of Psychosocial Development: Adolescence | **Survey**<br>The Best Age to Be<br>**Lecture**<br>Developmental Tasks of Early Adulthood |

# Skills

In Unit 2, you will practice the following skills.

| **L** Listening Skills | **S** Speaking Skills |
|---|---|
| Recording numbers<br>Listening for specific information<br>Completing multiple-choice items<br>Uses of *like* in casual speech<br>Summarizing what you have heard<br>Correcting or expressing a negative politely<br>Uses of *get* | Examining graphics<br>Using background information to make predictions<br>Reviewing predictions<br>Summarizing what you have heard<br>Combining information from different sources<br>Sharing your personal and cultural perspective<br>Predicting the content<br>Responding to true/false statements<br>Identifying who said what<br>Eliciting a conclusion<br>Applying general concepts to specific data |
| **V** Vocabulary Skills | **N** Note Taking Skills |
| Reading and thinking about the topic<br>Examining vocabulary in context<br>Building background knowledge on the topic<br>Guessing vocabulary from context<br>Considering different perspectives | Using space to show organizational structure<br>Creating a chart<br>Paying attention to signal words |

## Learning Outcomes

**Prepare** and **deliver** an oral presentation on a particular period of life

# Chapter 3
# The Teen Years

Look at the cartoon above and answer the questions with a partner.

**1.** Why do you think Jeremy wants to be 18?

**2.** Did you feel that way at 16?

## 1 Getting Started

The title of this chapter is "The Teen Years" – the years from age 13 to 19 – when we experience great physical and emotional growth. In this section, you are going to read and discuss some quotations about the teen years and growing up, and you will record growth rates for a typical American boy and girl.

### 1 Reading and thinking about the topic ⓥ ⓢ

**A** Read the following quotations.

> **1.** To an adolescent, there is nothing in the world more embarrassing than a parent. – *Dave Barry, American humor writer*
>
> **2.** Adolescence represents an inner emotional upheaval, a struggle between the eternal human wish to cling to the past and the equally powerful wish to get on with the future. – *Louise J. Kaplan, American psychoanalyst*
>
> **3.** During the first period of a person's life, the greatest danger is: *not to take the risk.* – *Søren Kierkegaard, Danish philosopher*
>
> **4.** The day the child realizes that all adults are imperfect, he becomes an adolescent; the day he forgives them, he becomes an adult; the day he forgives himself, he becomes wise. – *Alden Nowlan, Canadian poet*

**adolescent** = young teenager (age 13–16)
**upheaval** = period of great conflict and change
**struggle** = conflict, fight
**cling** = hold on tightly
**forgive** = not be angry at (someone) anymore for something he/she did

**B** Read and discuss the following questions with a partner:

1. Barry is expressing a stereotype (typical societal view) of the American adolescent. Are teenagers in your culture also sometimes embarrassed by their parents' behavior? Support your opinion.

2. What two conflicting wishes do adolescents struggle with, according to Kaplan? What does "the past" mean to a teenager? What does "the future" mean?

3. What does Kierkegaard mean? What kind of risks do you think he is referring to, and why would it be dangerous *not* to take risks as a teenager?

4. Nowlan refers to three stages in a person's psychological development. What event or personal change signals the beginning of each new stage? Do you think that everyone reaches the third stage? The second stage?

**C** Does your culture have any common sayings about adolescents or teenagers? Share them as a class.

## 2 Examining graphics ⓢ

Look at the accompanying pictures. With a partner, discuss what you notice about the relationship between age, height, and gender.

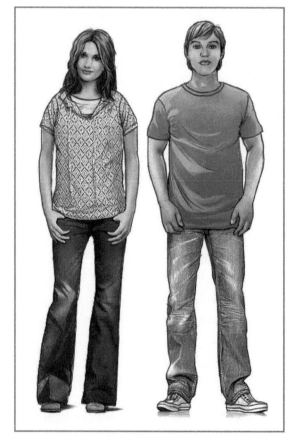

## 3 Recording numbers ⓛⓢ

Many listening tasks involve understanding numbers and writing them down quickly.

**A** Study the empty graph, where you will record growth rates for James and Sarah. Then listen and follow the speaker's directions.

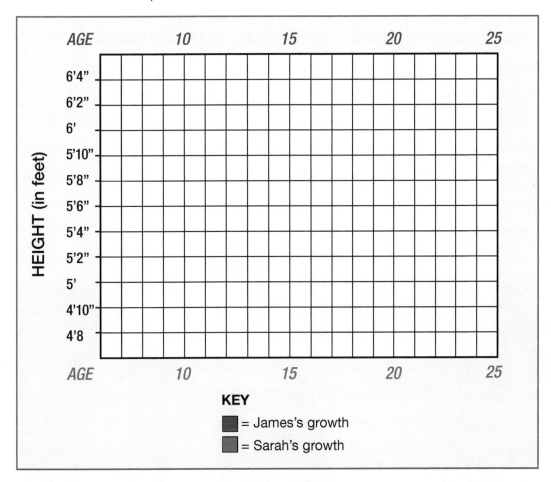

**B** Work with a partner. One of you will describe James's growth rate, and then the other will describe Sarah's. As you listen to your partner, check that you have the same information on your graph.

**C** Try to remember your own adolescent height changes and describe them to your partner. Were you ever much taller or much shorter than your peers?

# 2 Real-Life Voices

In this section, you will hear interviews with two 19-year-olds: Pegah from Iran and Anastassiya from Kazakhstan. Both are living in the United States with their families and learning English.

**BEFORE THE INTERVIEWS**

## Using background information to make predictions

> Finding background information about a topic and trying to predict what you will hear before you listen can greatly increase your comprehension.

**A** Read the following background facts about Anastassiya and Pegah.

**Anastassiya** immigrated to the United States with her mother and younger sister three years ago. Her father died when she was 12.

Anastassiya (right) with her mother and younger sister

**Pegah**'s father brought her to the U.S. to study English. She lives with her mother and older brother. Her father visits often, but works in Iran.

Pegah studying

**B** The teen years are challenging. What extra difficulties does a teenager face in a new culture? Try to guess what Anastassiya and Pegah will mention in their interviews. From what you have just read about them, do you think they face the same challenges? Use the box to write down some ideas.

## My Predictions

P & A both feel homesick.

_____

_____

_____

_____

**C** Compare what you wrote with a small group. Add any new ideas that you hear to your box.

## 1 Examining vocabulary in context ⓥ

Here are some words and expressions from the interview with Pegah, printed in **bold** and given in the context in which you will hear them. They are followed by definitions. Note: You may have already heard some of these expressions used in different contexts.

if you grow up with **this religion**: [in this interview] *Islam*

You**'re comfortable with** that: *accept, are content with, do not object to*

If it rings, you have to **pick up**: *answer (the phone)*

Pegah will be **lost without** (you): *completely dependent on; helpless without*

They **can't wait to** move out: *strongly want to, look forward to, are impatient to*

move out and **be on their own**: *live independently*

I need my family **to support** me: *protect, guide, take care of*

Is he **overprotective**?: *limiting a person (usually a child)'s freedom*

**Actually**, we already have lived together: *in fact* [used to show that what the other person just said or implied is not completely correct]

He ate it **anyway**: *nevertheless; even though it was not very good*

## 2 Listening for specific information Ⓛ Ⓝ Ⓢ

**A** Before you listen to the interview, read the following statements.

1. Pegah has lived in the U.S. for about _____ months.

2. Pegah says that in _____ , _____ usually do not go out without their parents.

3. When Pegah came to the U.S., she pointed out to her father that cultural rules in the U.S. are less strict, and she asked him for more _____ . He _____ .

4. Pegah's _____ came to stay with her in the U.S. because her _____ was worried about Pegah being alone. But Pegah's father has now changed his mind: He told Pegah that as soon as she gets her _____ her mother will _____ to _____ . Pegah feels _____ about this.

5. Pegah misses her _____ . When she feels sad, she tells her _____ .

6. When she is asked how American teenagers are different from teenagers in Iran, Pegah says that in her country, children live _____ until they _____ .

7. Pegah's father came to the U.S. to go to school when he was _____ years old. He was _____ , and he had no _____ . This experience was very _____ , but Pegah thinks it was _____ because it gave him _____ .

8. Pegah sometimes has disagreements with her _____ , who is _____ years _____ than her. But recently, their mother was on vacation in _____ , and he was very _____ to her.

9. Pegah's future plan is to be a _____ in _____ .

🔊 **B** Now listen to the interview with Pegah. Listen specifically for information that you need to complete the sentences in Step A. After you listen, complete them.

**C** Compare your sentences with a partner. They do not have to be exactly the same. Listen to the interview again if you need to.

# 1 Examining vocabulary in context 🅥

Here are some words and expressions from the interview with Anastassiya, printed in **bold** and given in the context in which you will hear them. They are followed by definitions.

They **canceled** the ESL program: *stopped, discontinued*

I **dropped out of** high school: *stopped going to*

You can experience **discrimination**: *not being treated equally by other students*

They don't **concentrate**: *focus their minds on a mental task*

They can **distract you** from learning: *cause you to lose your focus; take your attention away*

to **hang out** with Turkish people: *spend time with socially* [informal]

**There's something similar** in our vision of the world: *We are somewhat alike*

**vision of the world**: *world view, perspective, point of view, philosophy*

taking **regular** math class: *with native English speakers; not an ESL class*

You have an **interpreter**: *person who translates for people who do not speak the same language*

In Kazakhstan, I was . . . **carefree**!: *without responsibilities, without worries*

You had to **be in charge**: *take control, be the leader*

# 2 Completing multiple-choice items 🅛 🅢

Multiple-choice questions are the most common question type for language exams. They often focus on details in a reading or lecture, so read all the choices very carefully before you choose. Remember that sometimes the correct answer is "all of the above" or "none of the above." With practice, you will become more successful at answering multiple-choice questions.

**A** Read the statements and possible completions before you listen to the interview.

**1.** Anastassiya dropped out of American high school because _____ .
   a. her English class was discontinued    b. the American students were unfriendly
   c. she couldn't pass her classes in English    d. both a and c

**2.** Anastassiya says that in high school everyone is trying to _____ .
   a. learn as much as they can    b. be better than everyone else
   c. be kind to other students    d. both a and b

**3.** Some immigrant students from other countries were unfriendly to Anastassiya because _____ .

    a. she was from Kazakhstan
           b. she wasn't a good student

    c. her English wasn't as good as theirs
    d. all of the above

**4.** Anastassiya says high school students _____ .

    a. don't care about learning
          b. sometimes distracted her from learning

    c. are in school because their parents make them go
    d. all of the above

**5.** Anastassiya has now made friends from other countries, including: _____ .

    a. Turkey and Iran
          b. Mexico, Vietnam, and the Philippines

    c. Spain, the U.S., and Turkey
    d. both a and b
    e. both b and c

**6.** Anastassiya says that when she came to the U.S., she realized, "I'm not a teenager anymore!" This was because _____ .

    a. she missed her country
          b. she had to help her mother, who doesn't speak English

    c. she had to get a job to support her mom and sister
    d. her mother put a lot of pressure on her to be an adult

**7.** Now that Anastassiya is responsible for her mother and sister, she feels _____ .

    a. closer to them
          b. tired sometimes

    c. more equal with her mother
    d. all of the above

**8.** Anastassiya plans to _____ .

    a. return to Kazakhstan
          b. be a music producer

    c. be an artist
            d. both a and b

◀⅀ **B** Now listen to the interview with Anastassiya and complete the statements in Step A.

**C** Compare your choices with a partner and then share answers as a class.

## 3 Uses of *like* in casual speech Ⓛ Ⓢ

> Casual speech in the United States, as in any culture, contains expressions that do not appear in written language or in more formal speech. Certain terms, such as *like*, are especially common among young people. They can be used to *hedge* a statement (i.e., make it softer, less direct) or to fill time as the speaker is thinking of what to say next.

◀⅀ **A** The word *like* is used as a hedge in casual American speech, but it is also used in many other ways in English. You will hear ten statements made by Anastassiya. Listen for *like* and decide what it means in each statement. Write an X in the correct column.

| What *Like* Is Being Used to Mean | | | | |
|---|---|---|---|---|
| | A hedge or "Wait, I'm Thinking" | "As If" or "Similar To" | "For Example" | Verb to *Like* |
| 1. | | | | |
| 2. | | | | |
| 3. | | | | |
| 4. | | | | |
| 5. | | | | |
| 6. | | | | |
| 7. | | | | |
| 8. | | | | |
| 9. | | | | |
| 10. | | | | |

**B** Compare your results in a small group. Do you agree? Listen again if you need to.

**AFTER THE INTERVIEWS**

# 1 Reviewing predictions Ⓢ

Look back at your predictions about Anastassiya and Pegah on page 51. Discuss them as a class. Were your predictions correct? In some cases, you may have to conclude that you don't know. For example, is Anastassiya homesick? We don't know because she didn't say anything about it.

# 2 Summarizing what you have heard Ⓢ

**A** Pegah and Anastassiya are the same age, but they are different in some ways. With a partner, summarize verbally what you learned about them from their interviews. Use the words in parentheses as cues. (Note that for some of the items below, you may not have information for both Pegah and Anastassiya.)

   **1.** Position in the family (youngest / oldest / siblings / responsibility / independence)

   **2.** Relationship with parents (traditional / atypical / strong / loving / dependent)

   **3.** Other students in the U.S. (discrimination / language / attitude toward education)

   **4.** View of American culture (freedom / independent)

   **5.** Future plans (school / work / country)

**B** Share your summaries as a class.

# 3 In Your Own Voice

In this section, you will interview a classmate about his/her experiences as a teenager. First, read the questions in this mini-survey and answer *yes* or *no* for yourself. (Note: You will have a chance to talk about these points in greater detail later.)

1. In general, were your teen years enjoyable? _____
2. In general, did you get along well with your parents? _____
3. Do you have siblings? _____ If yes, did you get along with them? _____
4. Did you have any bad experiences as a teenager? _____

## 1 Correcting or expressing a negative politely Ⓛ Ⓢ

> There are a number of polite ways to let a person know in conversation that he or she has said something incorrect. Rather than say "You're wrong!" use a softer expression, such as: "Well, in *fact* . . . "

🔊 **A** You are going to share your answers from the mini-survey with a partner. First, listen to some excerpts from the conversations with Pegah and Anastassiya, in which they politely correct the interviewer. Pay attention to their intonation.

> **Polite Expressions Used by the Speakers to Correct the Interviewer or to Express a Negative**
>
> Mmm, not really, because our relationship was always very close.
> Well, *actually*, we already have lived alone together.
> A *little* bit . . . [in this case, = no]

**B** Work with a partner. Look at your partner's answers in the mini-survey and ask some questions. But make mistakes! For example, if your partner has written that she has no siblings, you could ask: *Do you get along with your brothers?* This will give your partner a chance to practice correcting you politely (*Actually, I have no brothers.*).

> **Some Additional Polite Expressions to Correct the Interviewer or to Express a Negative**
>
> Well, in fact, I . . .
> Yes, that is partly true, but . . .
> Well, I'd have to say, no, not really . . .
>
> Well, that's partly correct. Actually, . . .
> I can see why you would think that. But in fact . . .
> To tell you the truth, I . . .

## 2 Sharing personal information Ⓢ

Continue talking with your partner. Your purpose now is not to make mistakes and practice polite negatives, but rather to find out about your partner's personal experience of the teen years. Share something that you learned about your partner with the class.

# 4 Academic Listening and Note Taking

In this section, you will hear and take notes on a two-part lecture given by Susan Jenkins, PhD, a licensed clinical psychologist who works primarily with adolescents. The title of the lecture is "Erik Erikson's Fifth Stage of Psychosocial Development: Adolescence." Dr. Jenkins will discuss the challenges that adolescents face, and some ways in which those challenges have changed in recent years.

## BEFORE THE LECTURE

## 1 Building background knowledge on the topic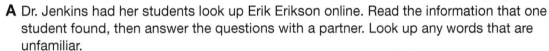

**A** Dr. Jenkins had her students look up Erik Erikson online. Read the information that one student found, then answer the questions with a partner. Look up any words that are unfamiliar.

**Psychologist Erik Erikson** (1902–1994) believed that personality develops in a series of eight stages. Erikson's theory describes the impact of social experience across the whole life span.

One of the main elements of Erikson's psychosocial stage theory is the development of ego identity. Ego identity is the conscious sense of self that we develop through social interaction. According to Erikson, our ego identity is constantly changing due to new experience and information that we acquire in our daily interactions with others.

In addition to ego identity, each stage in Erikson's theory is concerned with becoming competent in an area of life. If the stage is handled well, the person will feel a sense of mastery. If the stage is managed poorly, the person will emerge with a sense of inadequacy.

Erik Erikson

1. According to Erikson, how do people develop a sense of who they are (i.e., an ego identity)?
2. Erikson theorized eight stages of psychosocial development. What work does a person have to do at each stage?
3. According to Erikson, what happens if a person does not succeed in doing this work at a particular stage?

**B** Now that you know a little about Erik Erikson's theory, go back and reread the title of today's lecture. What do you think Dr. Jenkins talked about in her last lecture?

Now read the notes below, excerpted from notes taken by a student of Dr. Jenkins who attended her past four lectures. Look up any words that are unfamiliar.

Erik Erikson – Danish-Amer. psychologist (1902–94). In 1950 publ. *Childhood & Society* – 8 stages of development – each stg has a challenge to meet. Name of stg. = good or bad result: "___ vs. ___"

Stg. 1 – basic trust vs. mistrust (infant – abt. 2 yr old) – helpless baby must learn to trust that needs (e.g., hungry, cold) will be met. Mom's role very important.

. . .

Stg. 2 – autonomy vs. shame and doubt (abt. 2 – abt. 4 yr old) – toddler explores world – must be given enough freedom – not too much. Autonomy = toilet, walk, talk, feed self, able to say "no." Shame: "I am bad! Don't look at me." Doubt: "I don't think I can do it."

. . .

Stg. 3 – initiative vs. guilt (abt. 4 – abt. 6) - imitate adults – learn to dress self – new goals and desires – parents must encourage – if child not allowed to try new things → feels bad (guilty) for wanting to.

. . .

Stg. 4 – industry vs. inferiority (abt. 6 – abt. 12) school very important, learn new skills – develop physical and mental competence → self-esteem. Age ~12: peer opinions very important – "Am I good enough? Am I different?" Risk of feeling not good enough, inferior. Beginning of puberty – child may look phys. "adult" but still child.

. . . .

**C** With a small group, reconstruct the notes out loud. For example: *"Stage one goes from birth until about age two. The baby needs to learn to trust her mother or whoever is taking care of her. For example, if she is hungry, . . . "* Discuss any questions you have about the notes.

## 2 Using space to show organizational structure **N** **L** **S**

As you listen to a lecture and take notes, your goal is to understand the lecture and to produce a written record of what was said. But your notes should not be simply a list of the ideas presented in the lecture. They should also reflect the structure of the lecture: how the points relate to each other, which points are general, and which are specific.

As a note taker, then, you have to listen for two things at the same time: You must listen for the *content* of the lecture, and you must also pay attention to its *structure,* and record it as accurately as possible.

One way to record the structure of a lecture is with a formal outline, as in Chapter 1. But there is an easier way: When you take notes, you can show how ideas are related by your use of blank space on the page. List the general points along the left-hand margin of the page. Leave some blank space below each point so that it will be easy to locate these main ideas when you review your notes after the lecture. (You can also use the space to add details or explanation later on.) Then indent as you list the more specific ideas and examples. Continue to indent each time the lecture moves from more general to more specific, as shown in the following model:

> *The first general point*
> > *A specific point related to the first general point*
> > *A second specific point related to the first general point*
> > > *A detail about the second specific point (an example, a statistic, etc.)*
> *The second general point*
> > *(etc.)*

By using the space on the page in this way, you will be able to see the organizational structure of the lecture at a glance when you go over your notes. Your notes will be a useful tool for reviewing the information presented in the lecture.

**A** The following notes were taken by a student listening to an excerpt from Part 2 of Dr. Jenkins's lecture. Two points are very general. Three other points are more specific and should be indented. The remaining five points are even more specific and should be indented further. Read the notes. Be sure that you understand the abbreviations used. Try to decide which two points are the most general, which three points are a little more specific, and so on.

---

**Lecture Part 2 – Identity vs. role confusion – new challenges**

Drugs/alcohol, other mind-altering substances

Pressure to make decisions abt. use

Much research

Kids who use dr./alc. stop psychol./emotional growth

Drug = protective screen betw. adolesc. and reality

Chronic use → devel. stops

'Instant information'

Internet, Ipods, Iphones

Issue since TV invented: how affect develop. brain? we don't know

Comput./video games – diff. from TV: 'hypnotizing'

---

 **B** Now watch or listen to the excerpt from the lecture and mark which points in the notes in Step A should be indented.

**C** Compare notes with a partner. Did you indent the same points?

**D** Recopy the notes on your own paper or computer, indenting the points as you marked them. If you are using paper, leave plenty of vertical (↕) space so that you can add to your notes later.

# 1 Guessing vocabulary from context Ⓥ Ⓢ

**A** The following terms from Part 1 of the lecture are shown in **bold** in the contexts in which you will hear them. Work with a partner. Using context, take turns guessing the meanings. Hint: If you already know a word or phrase, scan the list of definitions in Step B below for the correct match and write the corresponding letter next to it. You can then mark that definition as already used; this will make Step B easier for you.

____ **1.** a conflict that the person **resolves**

____ **2.** The **establishment** of basic trust happens from birth until about age two.

____ **3.** the psychosocial **realm**

____ **4.** There are a few **components** to this work.

____ **5.** This is the time of **genital maturation**.

____ **6.** Kids going through this are very **self-absorbed**, worried about being socially accepted.

____ **7. in the midst of** this physical change

____ **8.** to establish an **ego identity**

____ **9.** able to **think beyond** their physical feelings

____ **10.** that they're gonna **make it through** this period

____ **11.** Lots of kids "**hit the wall**" a few times.

____ **12.** Another, **material** challenge that arises is making a choice about one's work.

____ **13.** a surprising amount of **anxiety** in the area of career choice for adolescents

____ **14.** All of that **comes** way **to the fore** during this period.

____ **15.** It's quite a **dramatic** change.

**B** Match the terms in Step A with their definitions by writing the letters in the blanks. Note that the definitions reflect the way the terms are used in the lecture; some of these terms can have different meanings in other contexts.

**a.** completely focused on one's self

**b.** process of developing something strong and important (e.g., a relationship)

**c.** not be controlled by

**d.** very surprising; very noticeable

**e.** becoming an adult sexually

**f.** sense of who one is

**g.** survive

**h.** have a bad experience; face a serious problem or crisis

**i.** figures out (e.g., a problem), finds an answer

**j.** becomes very important; is prominent

**k.** strong feeling of worry

**l.** area or topic that one is focusing on

**m.** happening at the same time and in the same place as; during

**n.** parts of a whole; aspects

**o.** concerning things rather than feelings or ideas; part of the physical realm

# 2 Organizational structure Ⓝ Ⓛ

**A** The following is an incomplete set of student notes for Part 1 of the lecture. The student has indented to give visual clues to the organization and content. Read the notes and notice how the lecture is organized. Try to predict what you might write in the blanks.

---

Lecture pt 1 – Adolescence: ID vs. role confusion

(adolesc = age _____ )

Primary work = _____

   If unable? → "role _____ "

       = cannot make _____ , know what _____

Components of adolesc work

   Challenge: phys & genital _____

       -Confusing for _____ because bodies _____

       -Rapid _____ e.g., _____ . (15.24 cm) in _____

       Result: adolesc very very _____ .

   Same time: social pressure from self and _____ to ' _____ '

       = establish _____ ,

       think beyond _____ ,

       keep basic trust: "I can _____ "

       Big challenge – many kids _____ ("hit the wall")

   Material _____ = choose _____

       Many kids postpone: _____

       BUT – most adolescs feel _____ about _____

 Falling in _____ → _____ ID

       Very _____ aspect at this period

       Related to _____ ID because adolesc faces new _____ .

       Dramatic change – can be wonderful or _____ - but always _____ .

---

**B** Now watch or listen to Part 1 of the lecture. Take notes on your own paper or computer. Remember to use symbols and abbreviations, and indent as the lecturer moves from the general to the specific.

**C** Use your notes to complete the student notes in the box; then compare your completed notes on this page with a partner. They do not have to be identical.

# 1 Guessing vocabulary from context Ⓥ Ⓢ

**A** The following items contain some important vocabulary from Part 2 of the lecture. Work with a partner. Using context, take turns guessing the meanings. As in the Lecture, Part 1 vocabulary exercise, if you already know the answer, find the match in Step B.

___ **1.** There's **tremendous** pressure in this age group.

___ **2.** drugs and alcohol and other mind-**altering** substances

___ **3.** There's been a lot of study of this in the last several **decades**.

___ **4.** emotional growth that comes from having to deal with experience **"naked"**

___ **5.** The drug acts as a protective **screen** between you and reality.

___ **6.** the reality that you are trying to **come to terms with**

___ **7.** They discover **to their shock** that they still feel 15.

___ **8.** This limitation of brain development is now **documented**.

___ **9.** ever since the **advent** of television

___ **10.** **on its face**, it's not a problem, but . . .

___ **11.** their first **true autonomy**

___ **12.** **It's not as if** they are trying to be careful.

___ **13.** They're *trying* to be **stimulated**.

___ **14.** They will **seek** stimulation until they have a problem or a car wreck, or . . .

___ **15.** new ways to become involved in stimuli that could be **harmful**

**B** Match the vocabulary terms in Step A with their definitions by writing the letters in the blanks.

**a.** real independence

**b.** understand and accept fully (usually something emotionally difficult)

**c.** very big; very strong

**d.** barrier; wall between you and something

**e.** look for; pursue

**f.** damaging; hurting you physically or mentally

**g.** arrival or invention

**h.** moved to react to something in one's environment

**i.** shown to be true by research

**j.** without studying it carefully or considering possible effects

**k.** periods of ten years

**l.** which surprises them very much

**m.** directly; without a protective filter (literally, "without clothing")

**n.** It would be incorrect to believe that . . .

**o.** causing to change; having an effect on

## 2 Organizational structure

**A** In Task 2 on pages 58–59, you heard excerpts from Part 2 of the lecture and worked on some notes on the excerpts that you heard. Read those notes again before you listen to the complete version of Part 2.

**B** Now watch or listen to Part 2 of the lecture. Add to your notes as you listen, and listen carefully for the conclusion. Remember to indent as the lecturer moves from the general to the specific. Use abbreviations and symbols to save time.

**C** Compare your notes with a partner. They do not have to be exactly the same.

# 1 Combining information from different sources ⓢ

Think about how Dr. Jenkins's lecture relates to Anastassiya and Pegah. Read the questions and discuss your ideas with a partner.

1. Anastassiya and Pegah are 19 years old. In your opinion, have they successfully met the challenge of identity vs. role confusion? Explain.

2. Does Part 2 of the lecture apply to Anastassiya and Pegah? Discuss why or why not.

# 2 Sharing your cultural perspective ⓢ

Discuss the following questions in a small group.

1. In the second part of her lecture, Dr. Jenkins points out that today's teenagers face new challenges: decisions about mind-altering substances like drugs and alcohol and the instant availability of electronic information. Do the same pressures exist in your culture? Discuss their impact on teenagers.

2. How has the experience of being a teenager changed since your parents were teenagers? Is life easier or more difficult for teenagers today? Explain your opinions.

# 3 Considering different perspectives ⓥ ⓢ

It is useful to hear a different perspective on a topic; thinking about an issue from someone else's point of view can help us clarify our own thoughts about the issue.

Read what American author and philosopher Sam Keen says about adolescence and discuss the questions below with a small group.

Adolescence is a modern invention, a time before the onset of responsibility. During this moratorium the not-yet-adult is allowed to rebel, to play, and to experiment. In primitive cultures, the son was cast in the same mold as the father. The sacred ways of the ancestors were repeated without alteration.

**moratorium** = a suspension of action
**be cast in the same mold** = follow the identical pattern; become like a copy of
**sacred** = honored; part of a culture's religious practices

1. According to Keen, how is a modern teenager different from a teenager in a primitive culture?

2. He refers to sons. What do you think he would say about daughters?

3. Keen implies that modern teens are not "cast in the same mold" as their parents. Do you agree?

4. If adolescence is a "modern invention," why was it invented, in your opinion?

# Chapter 4
# Adulthood

**that old** = as old as that person
**made it** = survived; succeeded in doing something

Look at the cartoon above and answer the questions with a partner.

**1.** What are the four people on the left thinking?

**2.** How does this contrast with what the man on the right is thinking?

# 1 Getting Started

The title of this chapter is "Adulthood." Like the teen years, adulthood is a time of growth and change – much of it personal and psychological rather than physical. In this section, you are going to discuss different stages of adulthood, and you will hear a survey of American adults of different ages answering the question "In your opinion, what is the best age to be?"

## 1 Reading and thinking about the topic Ⓥ Ⓢ

**A** Read the following passage.

The period that we call *adulthood* covers most of our lives. It begins with *young* adulthood, a time of many difficult but exciting decisions: What career should I pursue? Where should I live? Should I get married? What about children?

The years of *middle* adulthood bring other changes and challenges: Our bodies are beginning to show signs of age; our children and our parents are entering new stages of life.

Finally, *late* adulthood, too, is a time of difficult transition. Our bodies have slowed down. Friends, siblings, and spouses are getting sick and dying. Children have grown up and become independent. However, late adulthood brings its own rewards as well: Retirement provides time to enjoy grandchildren, hobbies, and travel.

**B** Answer the following questions according to the information in the passage:

1. What are the three stages of adulthood mentioned in the passage?

2. How does the reading describe each of the three stages?

**C** Discuss your own experiences and opinions with a partner.

1. The passage describes young adulthood in the United States as a time of decision making. What differences (if any) are there in the kinds of decisions that young adults have to make in your culture?

2. Do you consider yourself an adult? Explain.

## 2 Predicting the content Ⓢ

**A** How would you expect people of different ages to answer the question "What is the best age to be?" Complete the following chart with your guesses.

| I think that . . . | a man in his late 20s | would say that . . . | | is the best age to be. |
| --- | --- | --- | --- | --- |
| | a woman in her mid-20s | | | |
| | an elderly man | | | |
| | an elderly woman | | | |
| | a middle-aged man (40s–50s) | | | |
| | a middle-aged woman (40s–50s) | | | |

**B** Compare your guesses with a partner. Explain your choices.

## 3 Recording numbers Ⓛ Ⓝ Ⓢ

**A** Listen and follow the speaker's directions.

| Name | Age Now | The Best Age |
| --- | --- | --- |
| Bruce | | |
| Julie | | |
| Ann | | |
| David | | |
| Otis | | |
| Gene | | |
| Laurie | | |
| Loleta | | |

**B** Compare your numbers with a partner. Did you hear the same thing?

**C** Look back at your predictions in Step A. Did the speakers agree with you?

# 2 Real-Life Voices

In this section, you will hear the reasons given by some of the people you listened to in Section 1 for "the best age" that they named.

**BEFORE THE SURVEY**

## Predicting the content Ⓢ

Discuss the following questions with one or two classmates:

**1.** Why do you think Bruce says that his current years are his best years?

**2.** Why might Julie want to be a little child again?

**3.** Why do you think Otis says that his forties were his best years?

**4.** What might be Laurie's reasons for saying "My forties were *wonderful*"?

**SURVEY PART 1**    The Best Age to Be

## 1 Examining vocabulary in context Ⓥ

Here are some words and expressions from Part 1 of the survey with Bruce, Julie, and Ann, printed in **bold** and given in the context in which you will hear them. They are followed by definitions.

You **kinda** [kind of] know a direction: *more or less; somewhat but not completely* [a very commonly used "hedge" in informal speech]

You know how to **settle down**: *get a job, buy a house, get married, etc.*

**figure out what I wanna** [want to] **do**: [in this context] *decide what career I want*

You **pretty much** know what you like: *almost completely; more than kind of* [informal]

You're kind of **settled** into life: *stable; secure; in a more or less permanent situation*

**actually**, now that my sons are married: *a word used to introduce an opposite or unexpected fact or idea* [Compare this use of *actually* with how Pegah used it; see page 52.]

**when I come to think about** [or **of**] it: *an expression used when we change our minds or get a new idea as we are speaking*

## 2 Responding to true/false statements 🅢 🅛

> When responding to true/false statements, remember that a correct negative statement is true. Also, if any part of a statement is false, the entire statement is false.

**A** Read the following statements about Part 1 of the survey. Make sure that you understand the negative statements.

___ **1.** Bruce feels ready to settle down now.

___ **2.** Bruce says that in the early twenties you think too much about the future.

___ **3.** Bruce thinks that the adolescent years were the hardest.

___ **4.** Julie says that her childhood was not as relaxed as her mid-twenties.

___ **5.** Julie is trying to get used to all her new responsibilities.

___ **6.** Julie's parents don't take care of her anymore.

___ **7.** Ann felt settled in her thirties.

___ **8.** Ann changes her mind about the best age as she is speaking.

___ **9.** Ann does more things for her children now that she is older.

**B** Now listen to Part 1 of the survey. Write *T* (true) or *F* (false) next to the statements in Step A.

**C** Compare answers with a partner. Correct the false statements together. Now look back at your guesses about Bruce and Julie in Predicting the Content on page 67. Were they correct?

**SURVEY PART 2** The Best Age to Be

## 1 Examining vocabulary in context ⓥ

Here are some words and expressions from Part 2 of the survey with Otis, Laurie, and Gene, printed in **bold** and given in the context in which you will hear them. They are followed by definitions.

much more **receptive** to new ideas: *open; willing to accept*

Most of them **worked**: *were successful*

I got my **master's degree:** *graduate degree usually requiring two to three years of study*

free of my **commitments:** *responsibilities; things that a person has promised to do*

**'cuz**, I hadn't done that before: *because* [informal]

**The older you get, the more you think about your youth:** *As you get older and older, you think more and more about when you were young.*

What **an idiot** I was: *a fool, a crazy person* [informal]

when you're younger, **for instance:** *for example*

Your **joints** hurt: *knees, shoulders, elbows, ankles, for example*

## 2 Summarizing what you have heard Ⓛ Ⓝ Ⓢ

**A** Read the following incomplete summaries before you listen to Part 2 of the survey.

Otis is a retired university professor. He says that his best teaching years were between _____ and _____ because he was more open to new ideas, he _____ , and _____ . At the age of _____ , he created _____ . However, Otis feels that in another sense, his last _____ years have been the best _____ .

An 80-year-old professor giving a lecture

Laurie and Gene are married. They are both painters. Laurie remembers her _____ as a great time because she got her master's degree, she _____ , and _____ . Gene says that the older he gets, the _____ . Especially when he wakes up in the morning, he notices that _____ . He and Laurie talk about how long _____ . When he was a young man, in the Army, he used to _____ . But now _____ .

Artist in her studio

**B** Now listen to Part 2 of the survey. Complete the summaries.

**C** Compare summaries with a partner. Your answers do not have to be exactly the same. Were your guesses about Otis and Laurie in Predicting the content (page 67) correct?

## 3 Uses of *get* Ⓛ Ⓢ

> The verb *get* – by itself or in idiomatic phrases – appears with great frequency in English, especially in speech, and has a wide variety of meanings.

**A** Listen again to excerpts from the survey. In each excerpt, you will hear *get* used either alone or in a phrase. Complete each use of *get* by filling in the blank with the words that follow. Note: In one case *get* is used alone, so one blank will not be filled in.

___ **1.** get _____ teenage adolescent years . . .

___ **2.** get _____ things . . .

___ **3.** get _____ college . . .

___ **4.** get _____ having new responsibilities –

___ **5.** get _____ . . .

___ **6.** get _____ . . .

___ **7.** get _____ . . .

**B** Compare your completions as a class. Then match the meanings of the *get* expressions in Step A with their definitions below. Write the correct letter in the blanks at the beginning of each item above. Listen again if you need to.

a. acquire; obtain
b. survive and recover from
c. complete and leave
d. become

e. start doing something
f. rise out of bed in the morning
g. become accustomed to

**AFTER THE SURVEY**

## Creating a chart Ⓝ Ⓢ

Making a chart of the main points of a lecture or conversation is a good way to review the material, and it will also help you to remember the information.

As a class, recall what Bruce, Julie, Ann, and the others said about the various stages of life. Summarize the good points, changes, and challenges that they mentioned. Enter them next to the appropriate ages in the accompanying box.

| | |
|---|---|
| **Childhood** | *no worries* |
| **Teens** | |
| **20s** | |
| **30s** | *feel settled* |
| **40s** | |
| **50s** | |
| **Late adulthood** | |

# 3 In Your Own Voice

In this section, you will share your personal perspectives on the different stages of adulthood.

## 1 Identifying who said what Ⓢ

Work with a partner. Review the information in the task Creating a chart in *After the Survey*, page 70. Identify which person (Bruce, Julie, or Ann) expressed each opinion. For example:

**A:** *Who was it that said childhood was a time of "no worries"?*
**B:** *Wasn't it Julie? Yes, I'm pretty sure Julie said that.*

## 2 Sharing your personal perspective Ⓢ

Now think about the attitudes toward the various stages of life expressed by Bruce, Julie, and Ann. How are these attitudes different from yours? How are they similar? Do you agree or disagree with the opinions of the people interviewed? With your partner, take turns expressing agreement or disagreement with the attitudes that you summarized on page 70. Below is some language you can use.

---

### Expressing Agreement or Disagreement

I tend to agree with what (Ann) said about _____ .
I feel the same way that (Bruce) does about _____ .
My attitude toward the teen years is very similar to _____'s.
I share _____'s views about late adulthood.
I'd have to say I'm in agreement with _____ regarding _____ .
_____'s attitude most closely resembles mine.
_____ says that _____ is _____ , but I disagree / I feel differently.
_____ says that _____ ; I think I'd have to disagree.
I'd have to say I'm not in agreement with _____ regarding _____ .
_____'s attitude is most different from mine.

---

## 3 Eliciting a conclusion Ⓢ Ⓝ

**A** Now that you and your partner have expressed agreement or disagreement with the speakers' observations, you are going to ask your partner what she/he thinks is the best age (or the worst age) to be. You may already have a good idea based on the statements that your partner made. Use the language in the box on page 72 to elicit a conclusion from your partner.

### Eliciting a Conclusion

From what I have heard you say, I would guess that you think _____ is the best (worst) age to be. Is that correct?

Based on your statements, I think you would say that the best (worst) age is _____ . Am I right?

Would I be correct in assuming that you think _____ is the best (worst) age?

I'm guessing that you would say _____ is the best (worst) age. Am I correct? Did I guess correctly?

**B** As a class, compile everyone's conclusions. As you did with your surveys in Unit 1, calculate percentages. For example, if 11 out of 25 people picked adolescence as the worst age, that equals 44 percent. Which age did the most classmates consider "the best age to be"? What does the class consider to be "the worst age"?

Four generations. From left : son, grandmother, mother, and great-grandmother

# 4 Academic Listening and Note Taking

In this section, you will hear and take notes on a lecture given by Anthony Brown, a psychotherapist and professor of psychology. The title of the lecture is "Developmental Tasks of Early Adulthood." Professor Brown will discuss the important decisions and life changes that young adults have to make.

## BEFORE THE LECTURE

## 1 Building background knowledge on the topic Ⓥ Ⓢ

**A** In many academic courses, the professor will assign a textbook reading on the same topic as the lecture. Professor Brown wants his students to read Chapter 6, "Young Adulthood," in their textbooks before the lecture. Look at the description of Chapter 6 in the table of contents of the course textbook.

**B** Chapter 6 is about two major developmental tasks of young adulthood. The second task uses special terminology (intimacy vs. isolation) that should remind you of Dr. Jenkins's lecture in Chapter 3. Let's read an excerpt from the chapter that Professor Brown assigned to find an explanation of the term "intimacy vs. isolation."

> Influential psychologist Erik Erikson (1902–1994) theorized that the human personality develops in eight stages throughout life. These stages are not so much periods of time as they are a series of conflicts, or crises, that need to be resolved. [. . .] Stage Six: the crisis of *intimacy versus isolation.* If the adult has achieved a sense of identity, then she can form close relationships and share with others. Failure at this stage consists of being unable to relate intimately to others. The person may develop a sense of isolation, feeling there is no one but herself she can depend on in the world.

**C** Answer the following questions with a partner:

  **1.** Look back at Step A. What is the first developmental task that the lecture will mention? How do you think a person accomplishes this task?

  **2.** You know about Erik Erikson's Stage Five: *identity vs. role confusion*. What does the excerpt in Step B tell you about the meaning of *intimacy vs. isolation*?

## 2 Paying attention to signal words Ⓝ Ⓛ Ⓥ Ⓢ

As you are reading a text, you can *see* how it is organized. You can read section headings to guess the general topic, look at the paragraph divisions to find main points, and scan for signal words like *the most important*, and *first, second,* and *finally*, to get clues to the organization of the text. Most important, you can reread the text as many times as you need to.

However, in a lecture, you cannot hear paragraph divisions, you cannot scan for signal words, and you may not get a chance to listen to the lecture again. Fortunately, lecturers do use signal words like *first* and *finally*, and these structural cues allow you to hear how the lecture is organized as you are listening. When you can hear the organization, you can often predict what will come next, and as a result, your notes will be more complete and accurate.

You probably know the more common signal words – words like *because, however, as a result, so,* and *first.* But there are many other words and expressions that can act as road signs, helping you predict what kind of information will follow. Some of them signal that a definition is going to follow. Others indicate that the speaker is going to repeat a point. Some of the signal words that you will hear in a lecture are commonly found in both written and spoken English. But others (such as the expression, *as I said*) are generally limited to spoken English.

**A** Here are some important signal words, printed in boldface and presented in the context in which you will hear them in the lecture. What kind of information do you expect will follow each one? Read the descriptions below, and match them to the signal words by writing the letters in the blanks to the left of the numbers. You will use one letter twice.

_____ 1. **by** *developmental tasks*, **I mean** _____

_____ 2. supporting him- or herself completely – **that includes** _____

_____ 3. a different type of relationship . . . **that is,** _____

_____ 4. **the result is** that _____

_____ 5. **So, as I said,** _____

_____ 6. **But even though** it's natural, _____

_____ 7. **So we've talked about** _____

**a.** a contrasting fact or idea

**b.** a definition or explanation

**c.** details

**d.** repetition of a point

**e.** the effect of the facts or processes just described

**f.** a summary of main points

**B** Compare answers as a class.

**C** Now watch or listen to these excerpts from the lecture, and find out what information follows each of the signal words. Take notes in the blanks provided in Step A. Remember to use symbols and abbreviations. Do not write unnecessary words.

**D** Work with your partner. Use your notes to reconstruct orally what you heard.

**LECTURE PART 1** Separation from Parents

# 1 Guessing vocabulary from context Ⓥ Ⓢ

**A** The following items contain some important vocabulary from Part 1 of the lecture. Each of the terms is shown in **bold** in the context in which you will hear it. Work with a partner. Using context, take turns guessing the meanings.

_____ **1.** I'm going to speak about two of the major **developmental tasks** of young adulthood.

_____ **2.** This is the time for the **achievement** of independence from parents.

_____ **3.** Ideally, what's considered **optimal** is for the young adult to support himself or herself.

_____ **4.** be **capable** of supporting himself or herself

_____ **5.** supporting him- or herself **financially**

_____ **6.** a relationship based on **mutual** adulthood

_____ **7.** the sort of **culmination** of a long process of separation

_____ **8.** The current **economic** climate in the world has made that much more difficult.

_____ **9.** Even though it's natural, this is still a **crisis point,** when a child leaves.

_____ **10.** Change is a frightening thing for some people, but **there's no escaping it**.

**B** Match each vocabulary term in Step A with its definition below. Write the letter. Note that the definitions reflect the context in which the terms are used in the lecture; some of these terms can have different meanings in other contexts.

**a.** with respect to the management of money

**b.** it cannot be avoided

**c.** end point; conclusion

**d.** felt or agreed to by both people

**e.** things that one must accomplish in order to grow up successfully

**f.** the best; ideal

**g.** difficult period in life when one must make a change

**h.** accomplishment; successful completion of some task

**i.** able

**j.** concerning the production and management of material wealth

**C** Check your answers as a class.

## 2 Listening for specific information 🅛 🅝 🅢

**A** The following are incomplete notes for Part 1 of the lecture. Try to predict what information you will need to listen for. Pay attention to indenting, and remember that the points on the far left are the most general.

> ### Developmental tasks of young adulthood (Pt. 1)
>
> Young adulthood = from early or _____ s
>
>    in Western culture, young adult should be financially, _____ ,
>
>    & _____ indep. from _____ .
>
> 1st task = separate from _____ & create new rel'ship
> based on _____
>
>    – process really began _____
>
>    Financial indep: happening later in US today because of _____
>
>    indep: not always successful: _____
>
>    – crisis time because _____

**B** Now watch or listen to Part 1 of the lecture. Take notes on your own paper.

**C** Use your notes to fill in the blanks. Then compare notes with a partner.

---

**LECTURE PART 2**   The Crisis of Intimacy vs. Isolation

## 1 Guessing vocabulary from context 🅥 🅢

**A** The following items contain some important vocabulary from Part 2 of the lecture. With a partner, take turns explaining what you think each **bold** term means, based on its context. Even if you can't define a term completely, say as much as you can about it. Note: One of the words was used in the Chapter One lecture with a different meaning. Can you identify it?

_____ **1.** The young adult faces the crisis of intimacy versus **isolation**.

_____ **2.** The **theory** is that in adolescence, the child has developed a healthy ego identity.

_____ **3.** Healthy people during this period are able **to compromise**, to sacrifice, to negotiate, all of which one must do to make a marriage successful.

_____ **4.** able to compromise, **to sacrifice**, to negotiate, all of which one must do

_____ **5.** to compromise, to sacrifice, **to negotiate**, all of which one must do

_____ **6.** The ability **to adapt** to another person in this way will increase intimacy, or closeness.

_____ **7.** Other people experience this as **self-absorption**.

_____ **8.** They spend all their time in the lab, and their family is **estranged**.

_____ **9.** a fear of being hurt if they open up and are **vulnerable** to other people

_____**10.** It's difficult to give yourself in a relationship if your self is not **defined**.

_____**11.** With the divorce rate as high as it is, there is a certain **reluctance** [to marry].

_____**12.** a certain reluctance, a **skepticism** about marriage

_____**13.** marriage as an **institution**

**B** Match the terms in Step A with these definitions. Write the letter.

**a.** feeling of doubt; lack of trust

**b.** give up something that one really wants to keep

**c.** hesitation to do something

**d.** focus on one's self; lack of interest in other people

**e.** being alone

**f.** no longer having good communication; separated emotionally

**g.** discuss differences with the hope of coming to an agreement

**h.** come to an agreement, usually with both sides accepting less than what they wanted

**i.** be flexible, change one's attitudes or behavior to fit a new situation

**j.** idea developed by scholars in a particular field of study

**k.** custom or practice established by society

**l.** well-established; strong

**m.** able to be hurt; not protected

**C** Check your answers as a class.

## 2 Listening for specific information Ⓛ Ⓝ Ⓢ

**A** The following are incomplete student notes for Part 2 of the lecture. Read them and try to predict what information you will need to listen for.

Developmental tasks of young adulthood (Pt . 2)
2nd task - traditionally leads to _____
    *called "crisis of _____ "
    If child develops _____ identity as adolesc, → able to
    _____ in young _____ .
        – person must be able to compromise, _____ , _____ .
        – if successful → _____
        – if not succ. → _____
        – others see you as _____ , e.g. – scientist who
    _____ .
        – isolation is not _____ ; person is afraid
    _____ .
        – Success w/intimacy depends on _____ .
    Marriage in the West today: staying single longer
        – have freedom _____
        – skepticism _____
            → wait until _____ → much lower _____
    If young adults succeed at 2 tasks → _____

**B** Now watch or listen to Part 2 of the lecture. Complete the student notes as you listen.

**C** Compare notes with a partner. They do not have to be exactly the same.

### AFTER THE LECTURE

## 1 Applying general concepts to specific data Ⓢ

> A good way to check your understanding of an abstract concept such as *separation* or *intimacy versus isolation* is to try to apply it to some specific circumstances or data.

**A** Which two people surveyed in Section 2, Real-life Voices, page 67, are young adults? Do you think they both have successfully separated from their parents? Discuss with a partner.

**B** Read the following statistical data about changes in the American family, and answer the questions with a partner or in a small group.

- In 2000, 12% of Americans age 25–29 lived with their parents; in 2010, 15% did.
- In 2000, 5% of Americans age 30–34 lived with their parents; in 2010, 7% did.
- In 1970, the median age for men to marry was 23.2; in 2007, it was 27.7.
- In 1970, the median age for women to marry was 20.8; in 2007, it was 26.
- In 1970, 9% of women and 6% of men age 30–34 had never been married; in 2008, 24% of women and 32% of men age 30–34 had never been married.
- In 1970, the ratio of marriages to divorces was 3 to 1; in 2008, it was 2 to 1.

**1.** Do you see any data that supports what Professor Brown said about the process of separation from parents in the twenty-first century?

**2.** Do you think the data can tell us anything about *intimacy versus isolation?*

## 2 Sharing your personal and cultural perspective

**A** Read the following quotation from the lecture; then discuss the question below with a classmate or in a small group.

> Ideally, what's considered optimal is for the young adult to be capable of supporting him- or herself completely – that includes financially, emotionally, and socially.

The idea that we must separate from our parents before we can be adults is a Western concept, and it may not apply at all in other cultures. Does it mean anything in your culture? What expectations does your culture have of young adults?

**B** Share some of your thoughts as a class.

**C** You will recall that in his lecture, Professor Brown stated that adult children are separating from their parents later in life today than they did in the past. Read the cartoon. Look up any unfamiliar words. As a class, discuss how the cartoon relates to Professor Brown's statement. For example, what does the young man's father think about adult children living with their parents?

# Unit 2 Academic Vocabulary Review

This section reviews the topics and vocabulary from Chapters 3 and 4. For a complete list of all the Academic Word List words in this book, see the Appendix on pages 181–182.

## 1 Word forms

**A** Read the sentences and fill in the blanks with a form of the word. For verbs, use the correct tense and person. For nouns, use the correct number (singular or plural). Note: You will not use all of the word forms given.

**1. to establish, established, establishment:**

Ideally, the _____ of basic trust occurs in the first two years of life.

A young adult needs _____ his independence from his parents.

**2. theory, theoretic, theoretically, to theorize:**

Erikson _____ eight stages of psychosocial development.

In _____ , an adult is capable of making good decisions.

**3. challenge, challenging, to challenge:**

Some young adults are not able to meet the _____ of an intimate relationship.

Negotiating the period of physical and genital maturation is extremely _____ .

**4. to adapt, adaptation, adaptability:**

Forming a relationship with another person requires the ability to _____ .

_____ is a valuable quality to develop.

**5. to achieve, achievement:**

Some young adults do not _____ the goal of independence from their parents.

The establishment of ego identity is a major _____ for the adolescent.

**6. commitment, to commit, committed:**

Healthy adults are capable of making a _____ to another person.

Adults are able to _____ to something beyond themselves.

## 2 Topic review

Read the questions. Each question is followed by related words and phrases from the unit. General academic vocabulary is given in **bold**. Answer the questions with a partner; the words and phrases in the boxes will help you to recall the answers.

### Psychosocial challenges of adolescence

**1.** What does Erikson **identify** as the main psychosocial **challenge** of the adolescent **period**?

> **process** / **establish** ego **identity** / **role** confusion / **individual**

2. What **major components** are **involved** in this work?

> **physical maturation** / shocking / career / education / anxiety / gender identity / new **aspects** of oneself / **dramatic** change / **challenging**

3. According to the Chapter 3 lecture, what **specific issue** have adolescents had to face within the past several **decades**?

> mind-**altering** substances / **aspects** of development / effects are **documented**

4. What is a more recent challenge that adolescents face today, and how does it put them at risk?

> information **available** instantly / **computers** / **impact** on developing brains / **seek** stimulation / **normal** process / unknown effects

## Developmental tasks of adulthood

5. According to the Chapter 4 lecture, what is the first **task** that a person must accomplish to be considered an **adult**?

> Western **culture** / **major tasks** / **capable** / separation / **achievement** / **financially**

6. How and why has this developmental **task** changed in recent years?

> **challenging** / **financial** / **economic** / **establish**

7. What second **task** of young adulthood does the lecture discuss?

> **theory** / **period** / intimacy vs **isolation** / ego **identity** / **commitment**

8. What change in attitudes toward marriage has occurred in the West in recent decades, according to the lecture, and what is the result?

> **reluctance** / **institution** / single / divorce

# Oral Presentation

In this section, you will be asked to choose one particular period of life, describe it, and state both what is good and what is challenging about it – supported by evidence from interviews that you will conduct.

## BEFORE THE PRESENTATION

## 1 Conducting interviews

> Conducting an interview is different from conducting a survey in that you are seeking **detailed information** from a **small number of people** – sometimes only one person. Your questions can be open-ended because you are looking for long, thoughtful responses.

## 2 Presenting both sides

**A** As a first step toward deciding what period of life you want to research and present, talk briefly to as many people as you can, focusing on older people if possible (because they have more life experience). Ask:

> *What would you say was the best period of your life so far? What was the worst?*

Do not ask for details at this point. Your goal is to identify two to three people who appear to have strong opinions about **the same period of life**; they do not necessarily have to agree with each other because you will be presenting both the good and bad aspects of that period of life.

**B** Once you have chosen your topic and your interviewees, conduct your interviews. Remember to ask for details at this point; you will want specific examples for your oral presentation. Here are some questions:

> *What specific challenges did you face in your early teens/20s/30s/40s?*
> *What was difficult about that time of life?*
> *Can you give me an example of the difficulties you faced?*
> *What was especially challenging about your _____s?*
> *What was especially good about your _____s?*
> *Why did you enjoy that period of your life so much?*

You can either record the interviews, or just take good notes, as in the following example:

| Topic: Early 30s – good and bad | | |
|---|---|---|
| **Interviewee** | **Good Points** | **Challenges / Difficulties** |
| My mother | New job = > independence | |
| Mr. Alvarez | | Company closed – lost job |
| Maria | | Finished school but couldn't find job |

## 3 Organizing your presentation

You will notice that the chart above is organized as follows:

Early 30s → good points, bad points
However, all three people above mentioned **work** as an important issue, and it appeared in both the Good Points and Challenges / Difficulties columns. Therefore, a more logical way to present their information might be:
Early 30s – important issues → work (good points, bad points), etc.
Review the information that you have collected and look for common points, then decide on the best way to organize your presentation.

## Keys to a successful presentation: Defining terms and using signal words

**Defining terms.** When you speak, use language that you are sure your classmates will understand, and explain any terms that you think may be difficult to understand. For example:

*The 20s can be a time of **financial challenges** – uh, problems with money.*

**Using signal words.** One way to keep your audience's attention and improve their understanding is to provide clear verbal cues for what is coming next. For example:

*Family relationships can be a source of great happiness in the teen years; **however**, they can also be challenging. **For example**, . . .*

When it is your turn to give your presentation, introduce your topic. Refer to your notes as you need to, but keep your focus on your audience. Are they following what you are saying? Remember to keep your language simple and use signal words.

**AFTER THE PRESENTATION**

## Engaging the audience

As you are presenting the opinions of your interviewees, your audience is probably responding internally – either agreeing or disagreeing. After you have finished your presentation, invite them to express their opinions.

When you finish your presentation, ask your classmates to express agreement or disagreement with your opinions.

# Unit 3
## Nonverbal Messages

In this unit, you will hear people discuss nonverbal communication. Chapter 5 deals with *body language*. You will hear interviews with three immigrants to the United States, as well as a lecture on body language across cultures. Chapter 6 covers how we communicate via *touch* and *space*. The same three immigrants will discuss cultural differences they have noticed in these channels of communication. Finally, you will hear a lecture on three different aspects of nonverbal communication.

# Contents

In Unit 3, you will listen to and speak about the following topics.

| Chapter 5<br>Body Language | Chapter 6<br>Touch, Space, and Culture |
| --- | --- |
| **Interview 1**<br>Brazilian Body Language | **Interview 1**<br>Marcos: Touch and Space |
| **Interview 2**<br>Korean Body Language | **Interview 2**<br>SunRan: Touch and Space |
| **Interview 3**<br>Japanese Body Language | **Interview 3**<br>Airi: Touch |
| **Lecture**<br>Body Language Across Cultures | **Lecture**<br>Nonverbal Communication: The Hidden Dimension of Communication |

# Skills

In Unit 3, you will practice the following skills.

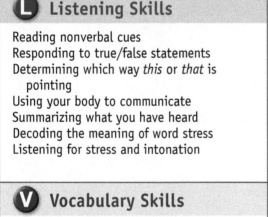

### L Listening Skills

Reading nonverbal cues
Responding to true/false statements
Determining which way *this* or *that* is
   pointing
Using your body to communicate
Summarizing what you have heard
Decoding the meaning of word stress
Listening for stress and intonation

### S Speaking Skills

Recalling what you already know
Thinking critically about the topic
Considering related information
Looking beyond the facts
Sharing your personal and cultural
   perspective
Personalizing the topic
Using comparison/contrast
Analyzing cultural content

### V Vocabulary Skills

Reading and thinking about the topic
Examining vocabulary in context
Guessing vocabulary from context
Comparing information from different sources

### N Note Taking Skills

Restating what you have heard
Mapping
Recording information
Reading nonverbal cues
Recalling what you already know
Summarizing what you have heard

## Learning Outcomes

**Prepare** and **deliver** an oral presentation comparing body language in two cultures

# Chapter 5
# Body Language

Look at the photograph above and answer the questions with a partner.

**1.** These business people are meeting for the first time. Describe their body language.

**2.** What do you think will happen next?

## 1 Getting Started

In this section, you will discuss the different aspects of body language and identify some common gestures used in the United States.

### 1 Reading and thinking about the topic ⓥ ⓢ

**A** Read the following passage:

Humans use language to communicate, but we also communicate *nonverbally* with our bodies. The way in which we stand or sit, how we use our eyes, what we do with our hands, as well as what we wear – all of these convey powerful messages to other people. In fact, anthropologists claim that only a small percentage of what we communicate is verbal; most of it is nonverbal.

Some of our body language is *conscious*; for example, we use the "thumbs up" gesture to signal "OK," or we frown to show that we are not pleased. But much of what we communicate with our bodies is *unconscious*: we are not even aware that we are doing it. Even in one's own culture, unconscious body language can be difficult to read. Imagine, then, how much more incomprehensible the body language of someone from a different culture would be!

**B** Answer the following questions according to the information in the passage:

1. With what parts of our bodies do we convey nonverbal messages?
2. What is conscious body language? Give an example.
3. What is unconscious body language? Think of an example.

**C** Discuss your experiences with a partner.

1. Think of examples of conscious body language used in your culture. Demonstrate them and explain what they mean.
2. Have you ever misunderstood the body language of someone from a different culture? Explain.

## 2 Reading nonverbal cues 🄻 🅂

> Always pay attention to nonverbal cues like gestures and head movements. They are a very important dimension of communication.

**A** Look at the gestures in the photos below. What message do you think each person is communicating? Discuss your guesses with a classmate.

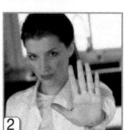

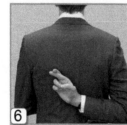

**B** You are going to hear eight statements. After each statement, find the gesture in Step A that expresses the statement. Write the number of the correct drawing in the blank after the letter.

a. ___     c. ___     e. ___     g. ___
b. ___     d. ___     f. ___     h. ___

**C** Compare matches with a partner. Did you get the same answers?

**D** As a class, go over the eight pictures. Do these gestures mean the same thing in your culture(s)? If not, what gesture do you use to express the same thing?

# 2 Real-Life Voices

In this section, you will hear interviews with three immigrants to the United States: Marcos, SunRan, and Airi. They come from Brazil, South Korea, and Japan, respectively. They will talk about differences that they have noticed in American gestures, facial expressions, and eye contact.

## Recalling what you already know ⓢ

**A** Think about the body language of people in your country. How much use do they make of eye contact, gestures, and facial expressions? Compare this with what you know or think about body language in other cultures.

**B** Complete the chart by circling a number from 1–5. A number 1 means a little body language, and a number 5 means a lot. Don't worry if you're not sure; just make your best guess. If you are from Japan, South Korea, or Brazil, leave the first line blank.

| NONVERBAL COMMUNICATION: Use of Body Language | | | | |
|---|---|---|---|---|
| | A Little | An Average Amount | | A Lot |
| People in my country use . . . | 1 | 2 | 3 | 4 | 5 |
| I think Americans use . . . | 1 | 2 | 3 | 4 | 5 |
| I think Japanese use . . . | 1 | 2 | 3 | 4 | 5 |
| I think South Koreans use . . . | 1 | 2 | 3 | 4 | 5 |
| I think Brazilians use . . . | 1 | 2 | 3 | 4 | 5 |

**C** Compare guesses with a partner. Discuss differences.

**INTERVIEW 1**  Brazilian Body Language

Brazilian soccer star Pelé talking with his hands

# 1 Examining vocabulary in context Ⓥ

Here are some words and expressions from the interview with Marcos, printed in **bold** and given in the context in which you will hear them. They are followed by definitions.

I wanted **to pick your brain**: *to get some information from you* [informal]

My eyes tend **to wander**: *to move around, to look in different directions*

I**'ve had people think** I wasn't paying attention: *sometimes my behavior causes people to think*

They **talk with their hands**: *use hand gestures as they are speaking*

observing how **seldom** people here seem to make gestures: *rarely, infrequently*

Brazilians **do indeed** talk a lot with their hands: *truly; in fact; actually*

because of an **unfamiliar** gesture: *unknown; not recognized*

**I wasn't doing any such thing!**: *You're wrong! I was not doing that!*

# 2 Responding to true/false statements Ⓛ Ⓢ

**A** Read these statements before you listen to the interview with Marcos.

___ **1.** Marcos moved to Brazil eight years ago.

___ **2.** According to Marcos, North Americans use more eye contact than Brazilians.

___ **3.** Marcos tends to look all around him when he's listening to someone.

___ **4.** Marcos noticed that his Italian relatives talked a lot with their hands.

___ **5.** Marcos says that people in the United States use their hands much less than Brazilians do.

___ **6.** Marcos's North American wife was confused by the way Marcos waved to her.

**B** Now listen to the interview. Mark the statements T (true) or F (false).

**C** Compare answers with a partner. Correct the false statements together.

**INTERVIEW 2**   South Korean Body Language

# 1 Examining vocabulary in context Ⓥ

Here are some words and expressions from the interview with SunRan, printed in **bold** and given in the context in which you will hear them. They are followed by definitions.

American **hand signals**: *hand movements that have a specific meaning*

the way you say "come," with your **palm** upward: *the inside part of the hand*

It means they are **interested**: *physically attracted*

**It's considered** more polite to stand still: *according to social rules, it is thought to be*

stand **still**, sit **still**, not move anything: *motionless*

It was kind of a sign of **bad manners**: *impolite or improper behavior*

I try to **minimize** that: *reduce; do less*

**How come** you move so much?: *why* [informal]

## 2 Responding to true/false statements ⓛ ⓢ

**A** Read the following statements before you listen to the interview with SunRan.

___ **1.** SunRan has lived in the United States since she was ten years old.

___ **2.** In South Korea, the American gesture for "come here" is used to call dogs.

___ **3.** When talking to an older person or someone with a higher social position, South Koreans traditionally look at the person's feet.

The subway in Seoul

___ **4.** Crossing one's arms is a sign of respect to older people in South Korea.

___ **5.** Between males and females, direct eye contact is a sign of attraction.

___ **6.** After ten years in the United States, SunRan's body language is still completely South Korean.

**B** Now listen to the interview. Mark the statements T (true) or F (false).

**C** Compare answers with a partner. Correct the false statements together.

South Korean students

# 1 Examining vocabulary in context

Here are some words and expressions from the interview with Airi, printed in **bold** and given in the context in which you will hear them. They are followed by definitions.

**misunderstandings** because of differences in gestures: *situations in which a person interpreted information incorrectly, usually resulting in bad feelings*

a **formal portrait**: *posed photograph for a special occasion like a marriage or graduation*

"Why didn't you smile?" "I ***did*** smile!": *English uses <u>auxiliary verb</u> (do/be/have/can, etc.) + verb to correct a mistake and emphasize that the opposite is true.*

this **gesture for "so-so, sort of"**: *holding the hand out with palm down and fingers spread, then rotating it to the right and left*

more than is **typical**: *usual; common*

I first started **dating** my husband: *going out with; seeing socially*

Airi (at left) at the wedding of her American sister-in-law

# 2 Restating what you have heard

**A** Read the incomplete paragraphs and predict how you might fill in the blanks.

Airi is married to _____ , and she has lived in the United States for

_____ . Airi discovered one difference in body language between Americans

and _____ when she saw herself in a _____ taken at her

_____ wedding. All of the people in the picture were _____ with their

_____ showing – except for _____ . She felt _____ when

she saw the picture.

Airi thinks that Japanese and Americans have similar attitudes about eye contact: In both countries, it's good for people to _____ when they're talking because it shows that they _____ .

Airi has noticed that Americans use more _____ than Japanese. However, Airi says that she is more like an American in this respect: She started using a lot of _____ when she met _____ because it was so difficult to _____ .

🔊 **B** Now listen to the interview, and then complete the paragraphs.

**C** Compare paragraphs with a classmate. They do not have to be exactly the same.

## 3 Determining which way *this* or *that* is pointing Ⓛ Ⓢ

**This** and **that** are a type of pronoun – that is, they act as a substitute for a noun or some other construction that is acting like a noun. What can be confusing about **this** and **that** is that they can point either backward (to a phrase or idea that was already mentioned) or forward (to something that will follow). For example:

*Body language varies by culture.* ←**That** *can be very confusing for foreign visitors.*

**This** *is what makes it complicated:*→ *Body language is both conscious and unconscious.*

🔊 **A** You will hear five excerpts from the interview with Marcos. In each excerpt, you will hear *this* or *that*. Listen and decide if the word or idea which *this/that* points to comes before (←) or after (→). Circle the correct arrow.

1. ← this → = _____
2. ← that → = _____
3. ← that → = _____
4. ← that → = _____
5. ← that → = _____

**B** Compare answers as a class. Listen again and try to write down the word or idea which *this/that* points to. Use the blank lines in Step A.

# 1 Thinking critically about the topic ⓢ

> Don't forget to evaluate the opinions of others in light of your own knowledge and experience. The ability to think critically is one of the most important skills for a student to develop.

We can make generalizations about body language, but it is important to remember two things:

- Body language is very complex and largely unconscious.
- Everyone's experience is different.

Read and think about these questions, and then discuss them as a class.

1. In this section you heard some generalizations about the use of gestures, facial expressions, and eye contact in the United States. What are these generalizations? From your experience and knowledge, do you agree or disagree with them?

2. SunRan and Airi have felt the influence of American body language. Whether or not you have spent time in the United States, has your use of gestures, facial expressions, or eye contact been influenced by American culture? If so, how?

3. What generalizations can you make about body language in your culture? If you are from Japan, Korea, or Brazil, do you disagree with anything you heard in the interviews? Can you add more information?

# 2 Considering related information ⓢ

**A** Read this list of body signals. To make sure you understand them, perform them for a partner.

- scratching the head
- shrugging the shoulders
- lifting an eyebrow
- winking
- tapping the fingers
- leaning forward quickly

**B** Body signals can have more than one meaning. The sentences in boxes A and B that follow give two meanings for each of the signals in Step A. One of you should look *only* at Box A, and the other *only* at Box B. Ask your partner questions to find the information you need to fill in the blanks in the sentences.

**A**

1. Lifting an eyebrow might mean _____ , or it might mean surprise.

2. Shrugging the shoulders might mean the person doesn't care, or it might mean

   _____ .

3. Scratching the head might mean _____ , or it might mean the

   person has an itch.

4. Tapping the fingers might mean impatience, or it might mean

   _____ .

5. Winking might mean _____ , or it might mean the person's not

   serious.

6. Leaning forward quickly might mean forcefulness, or it might mean

   _____ .

**Student A**
*What might it mean if an American lifts an eyebrow?*

**Student B**
*What else might it mean if an American lifts an eyebrow?*

**B**

1. Lifting an eyebrow might mean disbelief, or it might mean _____ .

2. Shrugging the shoulders might mean _____ , or it might mean the

   person doesn't know.

3. Scratching the head might mean the person is confused, or it might mean

   _____ .

4. Tapping the fingers might mean _____ , or it might mean anxiety.

5. Winking might mean intimacy, or it might mean _____ .

6. Leaning forward quickly might mean _____ , or it might mean the

   person wants attention.

# 3 In Your Own Voice

In this section, you will practice nonverbal communication, and you will interpret the body language of your classmates.

## Using your body to communicate Ⓛ Ⓢ

When you are in a foreign culture, the ability and willingness to communicate with your face, eyes, and hands is a critical advantage in making yourself understood by others.

We use gestures long before we use words.

**A** Listen again to what Airi said about how she communicated with her American husband when they first met. She spoke little English, and he spoke less Japanese.

**B** Now work with one or two other students. Decide together on a brief (1–2 minute) situation that you want to act out, and on who you and your partner(s) are. For example, you might be friends having lunch in a restaurant, and then arguing about who is going to pay the bill. The purpose is to communicate your story without words. Use your posture, your hands, your eyes, your face, even your voice – but no words.

**C** Now you are going to watch your classmates perform. As a class, make *conjectures*, or guesses based on incomplete information, about what is happening. Here is some language you can use:

---

**Making Conjectures**

I'm not sure where they are, but I think it's _____ .
I think it might be _____ .
It looks to me like they are _____ .
I don't think so because _____ is _____ . I think they are _____ .
_____ seems to be really upset/tired/excited/frustrated/_____ .
I get the impression that they are in _____ .
Now they seem to be _____ing about something.

---

**D** After you and your partner(s) act out your situation, confirm your classmates' guesses or correct them if they misunderstood. Use this language to help you. For polite corrections, review the language in Chapter 3 on page 56.

---

**Confirming Guesses**

You were correct when you said _____ .
Who did you think we were? _____ That's absolutely correct.
You were right! / You guessed it! / You're absolutely right.
What did you think we were talking about? _____ Yes, that was it! Well done!

---

# 4 Academic Listening and Note Taking

In this section, you will hear and take notes on a two-part lecture given by Ellen Summerfield, a professor of communication arts. The title of the lecture is "Body Language Across Cultures." Professor Summerfield will discuss the challenges of understanding the nonverbal aspects of communication in a different culture.

## BEFORE THE LECTURE

## 1 Looking beyond the facts Ⓢ Ⓥ

> Always look beyond the facts that you hear and read, and consider what they mean in concrete terms. One good way to do this is to relate the facts to your own experience.

**A** Read and think about the following quotations about nonverbal communication. Look up any words that you do not know.

> "[A]nthropologists claim that only a small percentage of what we communicate is verbal; most of it is nonverbal." – Introductory reading to this chapter, page 87.
>
> "[E]xperts in the field of communication estimate that somewhere between 60 and 90 percent of everything that we communicate is nonverbal." – Professor Ellen Summerfield, "Body Language Across Cultures"

**B** How can it possibly be true that 60 to 90 percent of all our communication is nonverbal? Work with a partner. Ask this question:

*"Do you like [any item or person]?"*

Complete the question with anything you want (e.g., *chocolate? football? coffee?* [*a particular movie actor*]?). Your partner will answer your question truthfully using **only nonverbal cues**. Observe them and tell your partner what you saw. For example:

*You lifted your shoulders and looked up at the ceiling. You frowned. I conclude that you don't like chocolate.*

Take turns with your partner.

**C** With your partner, read and perform the following two-line dialogue silently with as many different interpretations as you can (e.g., impatience, excitement, anger). Use nonverbal cues to convey the different meanings.

**A:** *Are you ready to go?*
**B:** *Yes.*

**D** Perform one of your interpretations of the dialogue for your classmates. Ask them what feeling(s) they thought you were communicating, and what nonverbal cues they noticed.

# 2 Mapping Ⓝ Ⓛ Ⓢ

When you are taking notes on a lecture, you want your notes to reflect the organizational structure of the lecture. You have practiced doing this with indenting. Another method of taking notes is called *mapping*. With mapping, you begin with the main idea near the center of your paper and draw lines out to related points. Mapping has several advantages:

- It gives a visual representation of the structure of a lecture and the relationships between the ideas.

- As you take notes, you can show connections between different parts of the lecture simply by adding lines.

- Mapping makes it easy for you to go back and add further details at any time during a lecture. This is helpful, because some lecturers tend to skip around as they speak and return to add comments about an earlier point.

**A** Study the following incomplete "map." It represents an excerpt from Professor Summerfield's lecture. There is one main point in the excerpt. How many supporting points are there? How many definitions?

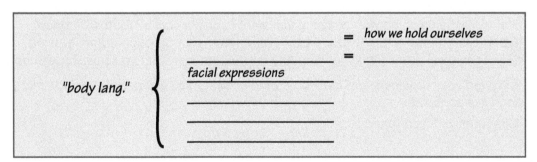

**B** Now watch or listen to the excerpt and complete the map. Listen a second time and fill in anything you missed.

**C** Compare maps with a partner.

## 1 Guessing vocabulary from context

**A** The following items contain vocabulary from Part 1 of the lecture. Use the context to choose the best definitions for the words in **bold**. Then check in a dictionary.

1. We're concerned about how the other person **interprets** our words.
   a. changes       b. does not believe       c. understands

2. **There is enormous emphasis, in all our interactions, on words.**
   a. We always use a great deal of word stress when we speak to others.
   b. We believe that the words that we use to communicate are very important.
   c. We think it's important to use gestures as well as words when we speak to others.

3. and our **tone of voice**
   a. voice quality (e.g., loudness)       b. how quickly we speak       c. pronunciation

4. Who has permission to touch whom, and **under what circumstances**?
   a. when and where       b. in what manner       c. why

5. After all, if we're learning another language, **what do we learn but words**?
   a. We do not learn words.       b. We learn only words.       c. We learn only gestures.

6. It's very easy to misinterpret these cues, or miss them **altogether**.
   a. in a group       b. completely       c. unconsciously

7. if you're **puzzled** by what's happening to you in a foreign culture
   a. confused       b. angered       c. interested

**B** Compare answers with a partner.

## 2 Mapping

**A** Study the following incomplete map of Part 1 of the lecture. Try to predict from the map how the lecture is structured.

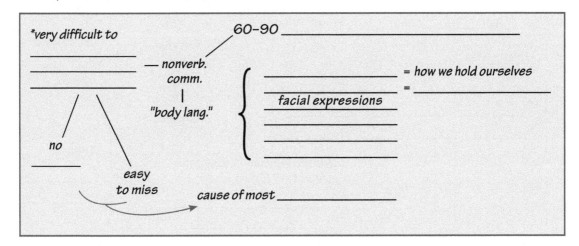

 **B** Now watch or listen to Part 1 of the lecture. Complete the map as you listen.

**C** Compare maps with a classmate. They do not have to be exactly the same.

# 1 Guessing vocabulary from context ⓥⓢ

**A** The following items contain some important vocabulary from Part 2 of the lecture. Use the context to help you choose the best definitions for the words in **bold**. Then check your guesses in a dictionary.

1. Looking directly into another person's eyes is **appropriate**, and if you look down, you may be showing disrespect.
   a. impolite    b. proper    c. friendly

2. I was paying attention to what was said to me rather than to nonverbal **cues**.
   a. answers    b. questions    c. signs

3. I have great respect for this **colleague**.
   a. supervisor    b. co-worker    c. employee

4. I know that he wanted to **cooperate**.
   a. be helpful    b. take control    c. disagree

5. I always interpreted this as a **green light**.
   a. warning    b. signal for "yes"    c. signal for "no"

6. It's so important if we want to understand the more **hidden** side of communication.
   a. not obvious    b. foreign    c. not polite

**B** Compare answers with a partner.

# 2 Mapping ⓝⓛ

**A** Study the following incomplete map of Part 2 of the lecture. Try to predict from the map how this part of the lecture is structured.

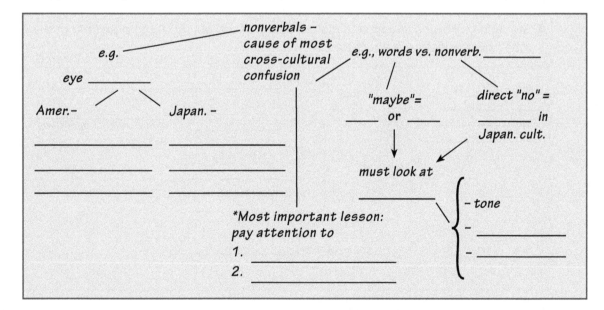

**B** Now watch or listen to Part 2 of the lecture. Complete the map as you listen.

**C** Compare maps with a partner. They do not have to be exactly the same.

## Sharing your personal and cultural perspective ⓢ

Discuss the following questions with one or two classmates.

1. You will notice that this chapter contains contradictory information about eye contact in Japan: Airi said that she noticed no big differences between Japanese and American patterns of behavior, but Professor Summerfield said that there is much less direct eye contact in Japan. What does this tell us about the rules of body language?

2. Think about eye contact in your culture. Are there some situations in which direct eye contact is bad, and others in which it is required? Think of some examples.

3. Is it sometimes (or always) impolite to say no directly in your culture? Can you think of ways that you express yes or no nonverbally? Compare notes with someone from your culture if possible. Have a short conversation in your own language, and try to pay attention to each other's nonverbal cues.

# Chapter 6
# Touch, Space, and Culture

Look at the photograph of the cricket players and answer the questions with a partner.

1. Does it seem strange that these men are hugging each other? Why or why not?
2. What other body language do you see among athletes?

## 1 Getting Started

In this section, you will hear and discuss how people communicate through touch and space.

### 1 Reading and thinking about the topic

**A** Read the following passage.

> We have seen that nonverbal communication includes use of facial expressions, gestures, and body posture. Two other ways in which we communicate without words are through *touch* and *space*. The cultural rules that control our use of touch (who touches whom? when? where?) and space (how close do we stand to our friends? to strangers?) are very subtle and largely unconscious. In fact, we almost never think about them until they are broken. Then we probably feel very uncomfortable, although we may not know exactly why.

**B** Answer these questions according to the information in the passage.

1. What two types of nonverbal communication will be discussed in this chapter?
2. Give examples of both types.

**C** Discuss your own experiences and opinions with a partner.

    **1.** Can you think of some examples of cross-cultural differences in the use of touch?

    **2.** What about examples of cross-cultural differences in the use of space?

# 2 Recording information Ⓝ Ⓛ Ⓢ

**A** Look at the incomplete table below. You are going to hear a short report that includes the information needed to complete the table. Before you listen, make sure that you understand all of the language used in the table.

**B** Now listen and complete the table. Compare your completed tables as a class.

**Zones of Social Distance for North Americans**

| Zone | Average Distance | | Notes |
| --- | --- | --- | --- |
| | Feet/Inches | Meters/Cms | |
| | | | |
| Business/social | | | |
| | | | |
| | | | |

**C** Look at the following bar graph. You are going to hear the information needed to complete the graph. As you listen, mark the personal distance that you hear for each of the cultures in the graph. Fill in the columns to create a bar graph.

**Personal Zones in Four Cultures**

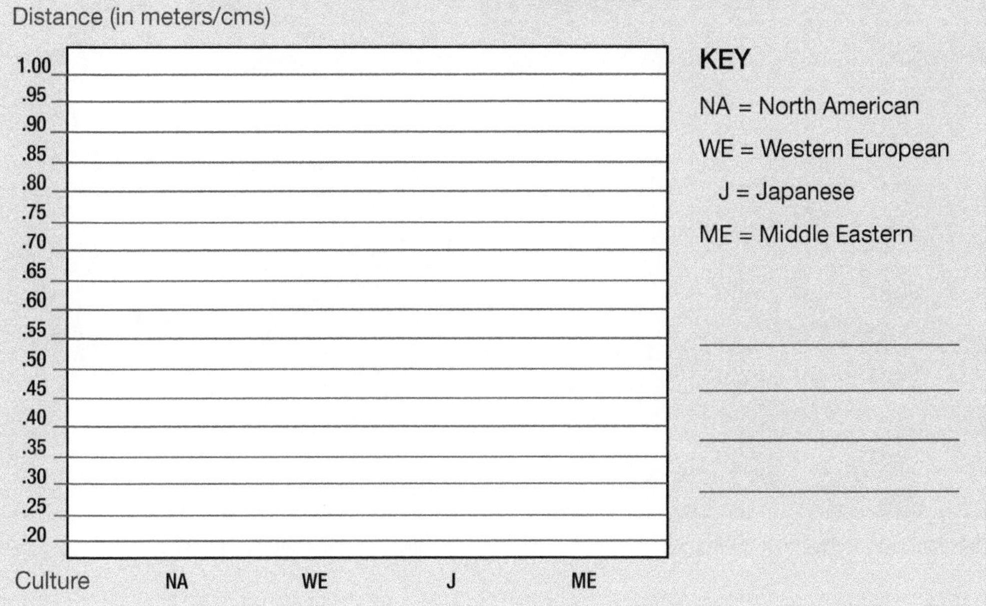

Distance (in meters/cms)

1.00
.95
.90
.85
.80
.75
.70
.65
.60
.55
.50
.45
.40
.35
.30
.25
.20

Culture    NA    WE    J    ME

**KEY**

NA = North American

WE = Western European

J = Japanese

ME = Middle Eastern

_____

_____

_____

_____

**D** Compare your bar graphs. Now measure these distances and try standing with a partner at the different distances. Compare how you feel at "Middle Eastern distance" and "Japanese distance."

**E** Study the pictures. As a class, discuss what zones of social distance you see, and what it means.

Sicilian friends

North Americans at work

A baseball player disagreeing with the umpire

Young European couple in public

# 2 Real-Life Voices

In this section, you will again hear the three immigrants from Brazil, South Korea, and Japan, respectively – Marcos, SunRan, and Airi. They will talk about touch and space.

**BEFORE THE INTERVIEWS**

## Recalling what you already know Ⓢ

**A** Think about the rules of touch and space in your country. How much do people touch one another, and how much distance is there between them when they talk? Compare this with what you know or think about the use of touch and distance in other cultures.

**B** Complete the following chart about the use of touch and space between males, between females, and between males and females in different cultures. Write numbers 1–3, according to the key. Don't worry if you're not sure; just make your best guess. If you are from Japan, South Korea, or Brazil, leave the first line blank.

| NONVERBAL COMMUNICATION: Use of Touch and Space | | | |
|---|---|---|---|
| | Between Males | Between Females | Between Males and Females |
| In my country | | | |
| In the United States | | | |
| In Japan | | | |
| In South Korea | | | |
| In Brazil | | | |

**KEY**
1 = a lot of touch and very little space
2 = average touch and space
3 = very little touch and a lot of space

**C** Compare and discuss your guesses with a partner.

## 1 Examining vocabulary in context

Here are some words and expressions from the interview with Marcos, printed in **bold** and given in the context in which you will hear them. They are followed by definitions.

He kept **backing up**: *moving backward*

I didn't really **realize what was going on**: *understand the meaning of what was happening*

this look of total **despair** on his face: *great unhappiness and discomfort*

invaded his **body bubble**: *the space around a person that no one should enter without first being invited*

Have you **modified** your bubble, your space?: *purposely changed to fit better in a new situation*

to **accommodate** us "cold North Americans": *make to feel comfortable*

**cold** North Americans: *socially reserved, distant*

**We were much more physical**: *We touched one another more.*

a little **self-conscious**: *embarrassed; afraid that other people are watching*

## 2 Summarizing what you have heard ⓛⓝⓢ

**A** Read the following incomplete summary before you listen to the interview.

Marcos remembers an experience when he was talking to a _____ of his from _____ . After a while, he noticed that the student had _____ into a _____ because Marcos kept moving _____ . The student obviously felt very _____ . Marcos had _____ his _____ . Marcos tries to stand _____ from people now that he lives in the United States so that they won't feel _____ . Marcos also finds that he and his _____ touch one another _____ in the United States than they did in _____ .

**B** As you listen to Marcos, complete the summary by filling in the blanks. Listen again if you need to.

**C** Compare your completed summaries with a partner. You do not need to have exactly the same words.

## 1 Examining vocabulary in context ⓥ

Here are some words and expressions from the interview with SunRan, printed in **bold** and given in the context in which you will hear them. They are followed by definitions.

**show** a lot more **affection**: *act in a warm, loving manner*

You'**re not supposed to**!: *shouldn't*

That **came as a real shock to me**: *surprised me very much*

They **hug** and kiss at school: *put their arms around one another*

**Young South Korean students**

## 2 Summarizing what you have heard Ⓛ Ⓝ Ⓢ

🔊 **A** As you listen to SunRan, complete the summary by filling in the blanks. Listen again if you need to.

SunRan learned to _____ when she came to the United States, but she

has to remember _____ when she visits _____ . She says that it

is not good for _____ and _____ to _____ in public in

her country. However, people of the same _____ can hold _____ .

However, SunRan has to remember not to do that in the _____ .

When she first came to the United States, SunRan was _____ by the fact that

_____ hug and _____ at school.

SunRan noticed some changes in _____ body language last time she visited

her country. For example, _____ , and young couples _____ .

**B** Compare your completed summaries with a partner. You do not need to have exactly the same words.

# 1 Examining vocabulary in context ⓥ

Here are some words and expressions from the interview with Airi, printed in **bold** and given in the context in which you will hear them. They are followed by definitions.

**Young Japanese family**

My family **would** never hug him: *would + verb expresses a habitual action in the past*

[not] hug him . . . **much less** kiss: *expresses a very strong negative – stronger than another negative in the same sentence [in this case, hug]*

I**'ve come to** understand his feelings: *have gone through a process of change, and as a result*

**Little by little**, I began to feel: *gradually, over time*

**It's rubbed off on** you: *it's changed [you] gradually over time so that now you like it [informal]*

She **was** just **accepted** to nursing school: *had one's application for admission [as to an academic or training program] approved*

# 2 Summarizing what you have heard Ⓛ Ⓝ Ⓢ

🔊 **A** As you listen to Airi, complete the summary by filling in the blanks. Listen again if you need to.

Airi says that most Japanese people _____ hug and kiss one another. Her

American husband felt _____ by this at first: He thought his wife's family

didn't _____ . When Airi and her _____ moved to the United States,

she was _____ at first because her American family _____ . But now

she _____ .

Recently, Airi visited Japan. When she met an old friend, she _____ . The

friend looked _____ .

**B** Compare your completed summaries with a partner. You do not need to have exactly the same words.

# 3 Decoding the meaning of word stress 🄻 🅂

Word stress is also considered a component of nonverbal communication: It is *vocal*, but not *verbal*. In spoken English, word stress carries a great deal of the meaning and expresses a number of different things. Here are three of the things that it can express:

STRONG FEELING: *That movie was* **so terrible!**
CHANGING THE SUBJECT: *I'm glad to hear your mother is doing well. How's your* **father**?
*Thanks, my father is well. How is* **your** *father?*
THIS (as opposed to THAT): *No, let's take* **your** *car (not mine).*
*No, let's take your* **car** *(not your motorcycle).*

🔊 **A** You will hear short segments from the interviews. In each segment, you will hear the stressed word(s) in the table below. Listen for the stressed word(s) and decide what you think the stress means. Write an X in the correct column.

| | Stressed Word(s) | Meaning of Stress in This Case | | |
|---|---|---|---|---|
| | | **Strong Feeling** | **Changing the Subject** | ***This* (as Opposed to *That*)** |
| 1. | touch | | | |
| 2. | male friends | | | |
| 3. | never | | | |
| 4. | you | | | |
| 5. | child | | | |
| 6. | now | | | |
| 7. | shocked | | | |

**B** Compare your answers with a partner. Do you agree?

🔊 **C** Look at the cases in Step A where stress expresses *this* (as opposed to *that*). Listen again and try to identify what "that" is in each case. Write your answer in the last column. You may have to infer the answer (i.e., the exact words may not be spoken).

**D** Compare what you wrote with a partner.

# 1 Personalizing the topic ⑤

Airi, SunRan, and Marcos all said that their rules for space and touch have changed since they came to the United States. Discuss the following questions as a class.

**1.** If you are studying in the United States, have your rules for space and touch changed, too? Has your body bubble gotten larger? or smaller? Do you touch people more or less than you used to?

**2.** If you are studying in your own country, have you met foreigners whose use of space and touch were different from yours? What were the differences? How did you or other people react to the differences?

# 2 Sharing your cultural perspective ⑤

Just as culture "rubs off on" individuals, cultures can also influence each other. Read and discuss the following questions with a partner, then as a class.

**1.** Compare the two photographs of people in South Korea on page 91. How are they different, and what do you think accounts for the difference? Do the photos confirm or contradict what SunRan said about body language in South Korea?

**2.** How has nonverbal communication changed in your culture in the past years? Think of specific examples. Why do you think it has changed?

# 3 Considering related information ⑤

**A** Read the following excerpt from an article on touch in *Psychology Today.*

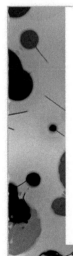

Touching has a subtle and often ambivalent role in most settings. But there is one special circumstance in which touch is permitted and universally positive: In sports, teammates encourage, applaud, and console one another generously through touch. In Western cultures, for men especially, hugs and slaps on the behind are permitted among athletes, even though they are rare among heterosexual men outside the sports arena. . . .

Graduate student Charles Anderton and psychologist Robert Heckel of the University of South Carolina studied touch in the competitive context of all-male or all-female championship swim meets by [counting the number of times that winners and losers were touched]. Regardless of sex, winners were touched . . . on average six times more than losers, with most of the touches to the hand and some to the back or shoulders; only a small percent were to the head or buttocks.

**B** Answer the following questions with a small group of classmates.

**1.** According to the article, in what context is touch considered acceptable? Is this true in your culture as well?

**2.** If you have seen American or European sports events on TV, have you noticed how athletes touch one another? Can you give any examples?

# 3 In Your Own Voice

You read in Chapter 5 (page 94) that body language is "very complex and largely unconscious." Therefore, in this section, you are going to do body language research not by *interviewing* people, but rather by *observing* and analyzing their (unconscious) actions.

## 1 Reading nonverbal cues Ⓝ Ⓢ

**A** Work with a partner. Choose two different groups to compare. It could be different cultures, different ages (e.g., middle-aged vs. teenage), or different genders (i.e., male vs. female). Then choose one aspect of body language to observe – either touch, space (proxemics), use of gestures, eye contact, or body movement (e.g., crossing arms or legs, touching one's head). Note: Choose something that you expect to see in the groups that you are observing. For example, if you are observing men in your culture, and men in your culture do not touch each other, do not choose touch.

**B** Once you and your partner decide what groups you want to observe, control for the other variables. For example, if you are observing people from different cultures, choose people who are the same gender and approximately the same age. That way, the differences you and your partner observe will be more likely attributable to culture (rather than age or gender).

**C** Decide how you will measure what you observe. Try to be as objective as possible. For example, if you are observing touch, you can count the number of times people touch each other within a certain period of time, and then figure out an average. Below is an example of a graph for observing touch. Your graph will be organized differently depending on what you are observing. Discuss with your partner and set up a graph or table to fit your choice of body language.

---

**Comparing: teenage couples and middle-aged couples (North American)**

**Body language being observed:** touch
**Observing:** teenage couple

**KEY**
x = female touching male
y = male touching female

| Time frame | Type of touch | | | | | | Notes |
|---|---|---|---|---|---|---|---|
| | **Hand touching ---** | | | | Arm around Shoulder | Hugging | |
| | Hand | Arm | Shoulder | Leg | | | |
| 3:05–3:10 | x x | x y | x y y y | | y y | | |
| 3:10–3:20 | | | | | | | |

---

**D** Choose a public place, like a café or park, where you can quietly observe people without being noticed for 30 minutes. Make notes and try to be as objective as possible.

**E** Now analyze your observations with your partner. What differences did you observe?

# 2 Using comparison/contrast Ⓢ Ⓛ

> The language we use to express how things are different and how they are similar is very important both in the academic world and in everyday conversation.

🔊 **A** You and your partner are going to talk about what you observed above with a small group of classmates. The language in the box will be useful for comparing what you observed. First, listen to the segments from the interviews with Marcos, SunRan, and Airi. Each segment contains expressions that compare or contrast body language in different cultures.

---

**Expressions of Comparison/Contrast Used in the Interviews**

Are there things that people in _____ **do differently**?
There is **a big difference**.
**That is not the way we** [wave / call someone / say yes, etc.] in my culture.
_____ **stand much closer** than _____ .
_____ **tend to use a lot of** _____ when they talk; in my culture we use less.
**In my country, it's normal to** _____ **but I can't do that here**.
**Are there any differences** in _____?
I think it's **almost the same**.
Americans **use more** body language.
That gesture for _____? **We don't have that** in my country.
The gestures are **different**, but there are also **more** of them.

---

**Some Additional Ways to Compare/Contrast**

_____ is a sign of _____ **in my culture**.
What **similarities/differences** did you notice in the use of [gestures / body movement / eye contact, etc.]?
_____ **use** their hands **a lot more than** _____ .
**There's a big difference** in the [size of people's bubbles / amount of touch / uses of touch, etc.].

---

**B** In your small group, take turns telling your classmates who you observed and what body language you were looking for. Summarize briefly what you noticed. Did anything surprise you? Compare or contrast the body language you observed.

**C** As a class, share part of the results of your discussion in Step B. For example:

We observed two teenage girls from _____ and two teenage girls from _____ . The girls from _____ tended to use much more body language and touch, for example, crossing their legs and touching each other.

# 4 Academic Listening and Note Taking

In this section, you will hear and take notes on a two-part lecture given by Mara Adelman, a professor of communications. The title of the lecture is "Nonverbal Communication: The Hidden Dimension of Communication." Professor Adelman will discuss nonverbal communication across cultures, focusing on the areas of *humor* (i.e., what makes people laugh), *space*, and *touch*.

## BEFORE THE LECTURE

## 1 Recalling what you already know

**A** Think of cross-cultural differences that you know about in the three areas that will be covered in the lecture. This may be information from the interviews or from your observations in this chapter, or from your own background knowledge. Record your ideas in the box.

| Humor | Space | Touch |
|-------|-------|-------|
|       |       | South Korea- ♀s hold hands in public |

**B** Share your ideas with a classmate. Did you get any new ideas from each other?

**C** Share ideas as a class.

## 2 Listening for stress and intonation Ⓛ Ⓝ Ⓢ

English speakers use stress and intonation when they speak, and these features can be as important to the meaning of a sentence as its grammar or vocabulary. Take, for example, the difference in meaning between "That's my cousin, Bill" (the speaker is talking to Bill about a cousin of the speaker) and "That's my cousin Bill" (the speaker is talking about his cousin who is named Bill). In spoken language, the difference between these two sentences is communicated through stress and intonation.

The stress and intonation systems in English are complex, but there are some general patterns that you can start to recognize (you looked at some uses of stress on page xx). In fact, these patterns can be especially easy to hear in lectures because lecturers often exaggerate stress and intonation to help students follow what is being said.

**Listing.** One common pattern is used when a speaker is giving a list. Look at the intonation pattern, indicated with arrows, in this sentence:

*This chapter focuses on humor, space, and touch.*

Notice that the speaker's voice rises on each word in the list up until the last one. Then it rises higher and finally falls to a low tone. If it does not fall, the speaker has not finished yet, or has not given a complete list.

**Contrast.** Another common use of stress and intonation is to show contrast. This use is similar to what we looked at on page 109: *this* as opposed to *that*. For example:

*Nonverbal communication is difficult enough to understand in one's own culture,*

*but becomes extremely complicated in another culture.*

Here, the speaker is contrasting "own culture" with "another culture" by using raised intonation and added stress (indicated with underlining) on another.

In general, English speakers use stress and raised intonation to draw the listener's attention to something important. As you begin to notice stress and intonation patterns more, you will find that they can help you understand the content of a lecture.

**A** The following excerpts from the lecture use stress and intonation either to show contrast or to give a list of words. Read them aloud and try to predict what intonation patterns you will hear and what words will be stressed.

1. "How much of those expressions are conveyed through verbal communication? More often than not, our intense emotions are conveyed nonverbally."

2. "More often than not, our intense emotions are conveyed nonverbally through gestures, body position, facial expression, vocal cues, eye contact, use of space, and touching."

3. "Imagine what would happen if you don't understand this bubble. What might you experience? Possibly discomfort, irritation, maybe even anger."

4. "It could express affection, anger, playfulness, control, status. . . . These are just a few functions of touch."

5. "In some cultures it is common to see same-sex friends holding hands and embracing in public. However, think about this behavior in some other cultures. Is it appropriate?"

 **B** Now watch or listen to the excerpts. Draw arrows to show the intonation that you hear, and underline stressed words or syllables.

**C** Work with a partner. Compare your marked excerpts. Then try to say each sentence with the stress and intonation pattern that you heard. Discuss what the patterns mean.

**LECTURE PART 1** Sarcasm and Proxemics

# 1 Guessing vocabulary from context Ⓥ Ⓢ

**A** The following items contain some important vocabulary from Part 1 of the lecture. Each of the vocabulary terms is shown in **bold**, in the context in which it occurs. Work with a partner. Using context, take turns guessing the meanings. Even if you can't define a term completely, say as much as you can about it.

\_\_\_ **1.** the "hidden **dimension**" of communication

\_\_\_ **2.** More often than not, our **intense** emotions are conveyed nonverbally.

\_\_\_ **3.** In humor and **sarcasm**, the verbal message is only a small part of the message.

\_\_\_ **4.** and similarly, when Americans go **abroad**

\_\_\_ **5. Proxemics** refers to our personal space.

\_\_\_ **6.** Body bubbles are very interesting because they're very **subtle**; you hardly ever recognize them.

\_\_\_ **7.** When someone **violates** your private space, you are suddenly conscious of the bubble.

\_\_\_ **8.** What is the social **context** – a party or a bus?

**B** Match each vocabulary term in Step A with its definition below. Write the letter.

**a.** to another country
**b.** study of how people communicate through the use of space
**c.** saying the opposite of what one means, often to show annoyance or contempt
**d.** breaks in; enters illegally or without permission
**e.** very strong
**f.** aspect; part of a larger issue or situation
**g.** difficult to notice; not obvious
**h.** situation in which something occurs

**C** Compare matches with a partner.

## 2 Summarizing what you have heard Ⓝ

**A** Read the following incomplete summary of Part 1 of the lecture. Remember that a summary includes only the main points of the lecture and may use different words from those used by the lecturer.

**"Nonverbal Language: The Hidden Dimension of Communication," Part 1**

Strong emotions are usually conveyed _____ : by gestures, body posture,

_____ , voice, eye contact, _____ , and _____ .

Sometimes we rely completely on _____ to communicate. At other

times, nonverbal cues add to the meaning of the _____ that we use.

One good example of the second case is seen in our use of _____ and

_____ . Often, in making a joke, Americans will say the opposite of what

they mean. The only way to know what they really mean is to _____

the _____ cues that go along with their words. These could be their

_____ or a _____ expression.

An important area of communication is *proxemics,* the study of _____ .

Each of us has a "_____" around us. Its size depends on several factors,

such as _____ , the social context, and our _____ . If someone

enters our _____ , we will _____ . _____ also plays an

important role in proxemics; some cultures – for example, _____ have smaller

bubbles than others.

**B** Now watch or listen to Part 1 of the lecture. Take notes on your own paper. Use indenting or mapping – whichever works better for you.

**C** Use your notes to complete the summary in Step A. Then compare summaries with a partner. They do not have to be exactly the same.

**LECTURE PART 2** Touch

## 1 Guessing vocabulary from context Ⓥ Ⓢ

**A** The following items contain some important vocabulary from Part 2 of the lecture. Each of the vocabulary terms is shown in **bold,** in the context in which it occurs. Work with a partner. Using context, take turns guessing the meanings. Even if you can't define a term completely, say as much as you can about it.

____ **1.** Touch is one of the most sensitive areas because touch is never **neutral**.

____ **2.** Shaking hands seems almost a **ritual**.

____ **3.** Think about some of the **functions** of touch; what could it express?

___ 4. It could express affection, anger, playfulness, control, **status**. . . .

___ 5. Is it appropriate? Could it be **taboo**?

___ 6. I decided to **incorporate** the same habit when I came back.

___ 7. We felt very **awkward** about it, and we stopped doing it.

___ 8. The **norms** for touching are very powerful.

___ 9. serious misinterpretations or anger or **alienation**

___ 10. the source of a lot of humor and **camaraderie** between people

**B** Match each vocabulary term in Step A with its definition below. Write the letter.

**a.** uncomfortable
**b.** warmth; friendliness
**c.** socially wrong
**d.** start using
**e.** feeling of being an outsider; social isolation
**f.** social habit, often done without much thought
**g.** social rules
**h.** neither positive nor negative
**i.** social position relative to other people
**j.** uses, purposes

**C** Compare answers with a partner.

## 2 Summarizing what you have heard Ⓝ Ⓛ Ⓢ

**A** Read the following incomplete summary of Part 2 of the lecture.

**"Nonverbal Language: The Hidden Dimension of Communication," Part 2**

Another important form of _____ is _____ . As with space, rules of _____ are very subtle, and they are mostly determined by _____ and _____ . What is acceptable in one culture may be _____ in another culture. For example, in China, _____ . But in the United States, _____ .

In conclusion, we should remember that nonverbal _____ do not often result in cross-cultural _____ . In fact, these mistakes can be a source of _____ and _____ between people of different cultures.

🔊 **B** Now watch or listen to Part 2 of the lecture. Take notes on your own paper. Use indenting or mapping – whichever works better for you.

**C** Use your notes to complete the summary in Step A. Then compare summaries with a partner. They will probably not be exactly the same.

# 1 Analyzing cultural content Ⓢ

What makes people laugh? Humor, like language, is culture-specific, and has to be learned in the same way that a different language is learned. Analyzing humor in another culture – for example, in cartoons — can give you a deeper understanding of the culture.

**A** Read the cartoon aloud with a partner. Be sure to use the word stress shown in **bold** and imitate the body language that you see in the drawings.

Zits

MOM, IF I'M OLD ENOUGH TO DRIVE, WHY DO I HAVE TO TELL YOU EVERY SINGLE PLACE I'M GOING?

BECAUSE IT MAKES ME FEEL BETTER.

**OH!** SO IT'S OKAY FOR ME TO LOOK LIKE A TOTAL DORK AS LONG AS IT MAKES **YOU** FEEL BETTER??

YES.

WELL, AT LEAST THIS EXPLAINS DAD.

HAVE A NICE DRIVE!

**look like a total dork:** (slang) be judged by one's peers as "dorky," not "cool"

**B** Answer these questions in a small group.

**1.** Professor Adelman talked about the use of sarcasm. Review the meaning of sarcasm.

**2.** Can you identify an example of sarcasm in the cartoon? Why is the speaker using sarcasm?

**3.** Does your culture use sarcasm? Think of examples.

# 2 Sharing your personal and cultural perspective Ⓢ

Discuss the following questions in a small group:

**1.** Have you had difficulty understanding humor in another language? Talk about why jokes are difficult to understand across cultures. Think of a joke in your language and tell it – in English to your teacher or to a classmate from a different country if possible. Did the person laugh? Did you need to explain it?

**2.** When she tried to hold hands with her sister in the United States, the lecturer found that she felt too embarrassed – that cultural norms for touching are too powerful to ignore. If you have ever lived in a foreign country, have you experienced surprise or embarrassment at differences in the norms of touching?

**3.** Do you have questions about anything that you heard in the lecture? Is there anything that you disagree with? Discuss these points with your group and teacher.

## 3 Comparing information from different sources

**A** Read the following article about an experiment using proxemics. Look up any words that you do not know.

### How much room does a person need?

Julius Fast, who is a major authority on body language, described an event which turned out to be an important lesson in body language.

Fast was in a restaurant, sitting at a table having lunch with a psychiatrist friend of his. They were sitting opposite each other at a table for two. His friend took a pack of cigarettes from his pocket, lit one and laid the pack just in front of Fast's place setting while continuing to talk.

Fast found that he was uncomfortable, but was not able to understand why. This uneasiness increased when the friend pushed his place setting toward the packet of cigarettes. When the friend then leaned forward over the table directly towards him, Fast felt so irritated that he had to interrupt the conversation.

Then his friend leaned back and said smiling:

"I have demonstrated to you a basic fact of body language. Initially, I pushed my cigarette packet towards you. We had already divided the table into two, on the basis of established convention: one half for me and the other for you. In imagination, we had marked our territories. Normally, we should have politely divided the table into two and respected the other's half. I put my cigarettes deliberately into your half, and thereby broke the agreement. Although you did not know what I was doing, you felt uneasy. When I made another move into your territory, pushing my plate and silverware forward, and then finally leaned forward myself, you were feeling more and more uncomfortable and threatened, but you still did not know why."

What Fast is describing is the classic reaction to a threat to one's territory that we experience when our personal space is invaded.

**B** Read and discuss these questions as a class.

1. Recall the interviews you heard in this chapter. Which interview had a similar event?

2. Which photo in this chapter shows someone threatening a person's territory?

3. Why do you think Julius Fast's friend conducted this experiment on him? What, if anything, is surprising about Fast's reaction?

Diagram showing how Fast's friend invaded his personal space

**C** On your own, duplicate the psychiatrist's experiment with a friend or family member. Pay attention to his/her reaction, and then explain what you were doing. As a class, share the reactions you received. Were they upset?

# Unit 3 Academic Vocabulary Review

This section reviews the vocabulary from Chapters 5 and 6. For a complete list of all the Academic Word List words in this book, see the Appendix on pages 181–182.

## 1 Word forms

Read the sentences and fill in the blanks with a form of the word. For nouns, use the correct number (singular or plural). For verbs, use the correct tense and person. Note: You will not use all of the word forms given.

**1. to communicate, communication, communicative:**

A large part of what we _____ is nonverbal.

Nonverbal _____ is subtle and complex.

**2. to emphasize, emphasis, emphatic:**

Experts in nonverbal communication _____ that body language is unconscious.

As language learners, we place a lot of _____ on the meaning of words.

**3. to interpret, to misinterpret, interpretation, misinterpretation, interpretive:**

The correct _____ of a gesture depends on context.

The lecturer _____ a Japanese speaker's use of *maybe* as *yes*.

_____ of body language is not at all unusual in cross-cultural situations.

**4. to function, function, functional:**

Gestures serve an important _____ in communication across cultures.

The _____ role of space was studied extensively by Edward T. Hall.

**5. dimension, dimensional:**

Interpersonal communication includes several _____ .

A multi-_____ study of communication would consider both its verbal and nonverbal aspects.

**6. intense, intensity, to intensify:**

Facial expressions can _____ the power of our words.

Use of direct eye contact adds to the _____ of a face-to-face interaction.

The emotional connection between two people becomes less _____ as their physical distance increases.

**7. to violate, violation:**

A person may unknowingly _____ a social norm in another culture.

The _____ of our personal space, or "body bubble," can create great psychological discomfort.

**8. to contextualize, context, contextual**

It's important to learn to pay attention to _____ cues in a foreign culture.

Touch can be acceptable or inappropriate, depending on the _____ in which it occurs.

**9. complexity, complex:**

Anyone who is married to a person from a different culture knows how _____ nonverbal communication can be.

The more time we spend in another culture, the better we understand its _____ .

10. **norm, normal, abnormal:**

The _____ of nonverbal communication are, for the most part, learned unconsciously.

Behavior that is considered _____ in one situation may be completely unacceptable in another context.

# 2 Topic review

Read the questions. Each question is followed by a box containing related words and phrases from the unit. General academic vocabulary is given in **bold**. Answer the questions with a partner; the words and phrases in the boxes will help you to recall the answers.

## Nonverbal communication

1. How big a **role** does nonverbal **communication** play in human **interactions**?

> **estimate / percent**

2. What are the different **components** of nonverbal **communication**? Demonstrate them.

> eye **contact** / gestures / **posture** / facial expressions / touch / body movement / **area** of proxemics

## Body language and culture

3. What is the relationship between body language and **culture**? Give examples.

> **context** / unconscious / **interpret** / **specific** meaning

4. How does the use of the different components (see 2 above) of body language vary by **culture**? Discuss each and give examples.

> different **norms** / social **context** / **status** / **appropriate**

5. What are some cross-**cultural** problems that can arise in the use of gestures? Give examples from the unit or from your own experience.

> **misinterpret** / **inappropriate** / **interactions** / social **context** / **status** / **violate** social **norms**

6. Stress and intonation are also part of nonverbal **communication**. Why is it important to pay attention to these in a foreign **culture**?

> **misinterpret** / sarcasm / stress and intonation / **source** of **miscommunication**

7. What effect does cross-**cultural** contact have on a person's system of nonverbal **communication**?

> **communication** / **modify** / **incorporate** gestures

# Oral Presentation

In this section, you will have the opportunity to educate your classmates about your own culture's body language by comparing it with that of another culture with which you are familiar.

## 1 Deciding on a topic

You are going to compare and contrast your own culture's body language with that of another culture, so choose another culture that you know well, and be prepared to do some further research on it if needed. Do not try to cover all of the areas of body language (i.e., facial expressions, gestures, body movement, eye contact, proxemics, and touch). Rather, choose two or three areas that you feel most qualified to discuss.

## 2 Gathering information

**A** When you have decided what aspects of nonverbal communication to talk about and which cultures to compare, review what you already know. You may want to use a brainstorming grid like the one below.

| Body Language | My Culture | _____ |
|---|---|---|
| Proxemics | People stand close together – esp. couples | |
| Gestures | | |

**B** Now gather additional information to complete your notes by observing people in a public place or by watching videos or TV.

## 3 Preparing your presentation

Your presentation will compare and contrast the body language of the two cultures that you are presenting. Review the language that you used to make comparisons in Chapter 6 (page 112). Remember to include examples. Write your main ideas on note cards and practice giving your presentation in the mirror or for a classmate.

Central Park in New York City. A public park is a great place to observe body language.

# Keys to a successful presentation: Monitoring your audience and getting them involved

Wow, this is a terrific presentation!

**Monitoring your audience.** You have been studying body language; now it's time to put your new knowledge to work. As you give your presentation, scan the classroom – especially the back row. What does your classmates' body language tell you? If they look uninterested, you may be giving too much detail. Consider moving on to your next point. If they look lost, slow down or ask if you can explain something again.

**Getting the audience involved.** Another tactic to keep your classmates interested is to ask for participation. For example, ask for a volunteer from your culture to stand up and demonstrate comfortable social distance with you, then ask the class for feedback. Or ask them to predict what you are going to say about, for example, the use of gestures in your culture compared to _____ .

When it is your turn to give your presentation, smile and relax! Everyone is interested in body language, and you have new insights to share with your classmates. Try to involve them as much as you can in the presentation.

## Giving and getting feedback

It can be uncomfortable asking your classmates what they liked and didn't like about your presentation. However, you will be doing the same for them. Two things to remember when giving feedback:

- Be constructive (i.e., give helpful criticism) and respectful. Even the strongest student can benefit from constructive feedback.
- Always begin feedback with a positive comment. What did you like? What did you learn?

When you finish your presentation, ask your classmates for feedback. Here is some language that you can use.

| Asking for Feedback | Giving Feedback |
|---|---|
| I would appreciate your comments/ feedback. <br> What did you learn? <br> What did you find most interesting about the presentation? <br> Do you have suggestions for how it could have been better? <br> If I gave the presentation again, how could I improve it? <br> Any other comments? | I really liked the way that you made eye contact / asked for volunteers from the audience / organized the information <br> I especially liked the part about _____ . <br> I learned that _____ . I didn't know that! <br> I think you could improve your presentation by _____ . <br> It was sometimes a little difficult to hear you / understand you. <br> You might try speaking a little more slowly. <br> You did a good job! |

# Unit 4
# Interpersonal Relationships

In this unit, you will hear men and women talk about the people who are important in their lives. Chapter 7 deals with *friendship*. You will hear an interview with a woman who takes her friendships very seriously, and a lecture on the meaning of friendship. In Chapter 8, on *love*, the author interviews a couple who have been happily married for 33 years. The chapter concludes with a lecture on what makes people fall in love with each other.

# Contents

In Unit 4, you will listen to and speak about the following topics.

| Chapter 7 Friendship | Chapter 8 Love |
|---|---|
| **Interview** Friendships | **Interview** Courtship and Making Marriage Work |
| **Lecture** Looking at Friendship | **Lecture** Love: What's It All About? |

# Skills

In Unit 4, you will practice the following skills.

| **L** Listening Skills | **S** Speaking Skills |
|---|---|
| Listening for specific information Retelling Listening for verb tense and aspect Listening for details Listening for digressions Showing interest | Personalizing the topic Drawing inferences Sharing your personal and cultural perspective Forming generalizations Considering related information Conducting an interview Applying general concepts to specific data |
| **V** Vocabulary Skills | **N** Note Taking Skills |
| Reading and thinking about the topic Examining vocabulary in context Describing a typical scene and typical activities Reminiscing about a typical scene and typical activities Building background knowledge on the topic Guessing vocabulary from context | Recalling what you already know Summarizing what you have heard Using morphology, context, and nonverbal cues to guess meaning Conducting a survey using the Likert scale Taking advantage of rhetorical questions Outlining practice |

## Learning Outcomes

**Prepare** and **deliver** an oral presentation on a famous friendship or love relationship

# Chapter 7
# Friendship

Look at the photograph of the ladies above and answer the questions with a partner.

**1.** What can you tell about these women from the photo?

**2.** What can you guess?

**3.** What might they be laughing about?

## 1 Getting Started

The title of this chapter is "Friendship." In this section, you will read and talk about what friendship means, and you will hear six Americans tell when and where they met their best friends.

### 1 Reading and thinking about the topic Ⓥ Ⓢ

**A** Read the following passage:

Friends play different roles at different times in our lives. We all remember how important it was to have other children to play with when we were young. During the adolescent years, so filled with physical and emotional change, we have more time, more energy, and perhaps a greater need for friendship than we ever will again. As adults, busy with our own lives, we depend less on our friends for support. However, friends still play a critical role for most of us, sharing our happy moments and helping us through difficult times.

There is a popular rhyme: "Make new friends, but keep the old; one is silver and the other gold." Most of us try to make new friends wherever we go – to a university, to a different job, to a new city – and we usually try to "keep the old" as well. However, maintaining friendships over time and distance is not easy. Americans tend to move around a great deal, and old friendships often suffer as a result.

**B** Answer the following questions according to the information in the passage:

1. What different roles does friendship serve to fulfill in childhood, adolescence, and adulthood?
2. Why is friendship especially important during adolescence?
3. Explain the meaning of the rhyme "Make new friends . . ."

**C** Discuss your own experiences with a partner.

1. The passage says that Americans often lose touch with old friends. Is this also a problem in your culture, or for you as an individual?
2. Do you have any sayings in your language about the importance of friendship? If so, share them with your class.

## 2 Personalizing the topic ⓢ ⓝ

**A** Work with a partner. First, think of a very good friend of yours. Tell your partner his or her name, and when and where you met. Ask your partner for the same information. Record his or her answers.

My partner's name: _____

His/Her good friend's name: _____

When they met: _____

Where they met: _____

**B** As a class, figure out how long (on average) you and your classmates have known the friends that you named. Where did most of you meet your friends?

## 3 Listening for specific information ⓛ ⓢ

🔊 **A** Listen as each person gives the name of a good friend. Draw a line from the first column (Speaker) to the second column (A Good Friend) to connect their names. Then write down when and where they met.

| Speaker | A Good Friend | When They Met | Where They Met |
|---------|---------------|---------------|----------------|
| Otis | Hubert | | |
| David | Odette | | |
| Pam | Esther | | |
| Tony | Tom | | |
| Catherine | Douglas | | |
| Ruth | Jeanette | | |

**B** Compare information with a partner. Did you write the same things? Where did most of the speakers meet their friends?

# 2 Real-Life Voices

In this section, you will hear the interviewer talk to her friend Catherine about Catherine's friendships – how they have started, how she maintains them, and why they are important to her.

## BEFORE THE INTERVIEW

## Recalling what you already know Ⓝ Ⓢ

**A** Complete the following general statements about friendship with your own ideas.

1. Some of the places where people first meet friends are _____

   _____ .

2. Friends are important because _____

   _____ .

3. In order to keep a friendship strong, you need to _____

   _____ .

**B** Compare ideas with a partner. Do you agree? Did you get any new ideas?

## INTERVIEW PART 1   Starting Friendships

## 1 Examining vocabulary in context Ⓥ

Here are some words and expressions from Part 1 of the interview with Catherine, printed in **bold** and given in the context in which you will hear them. They are followed by definitions.

What started it was when I **asked you a favor**: *made a request for help*

to give my cat a **flea** bath: *a very small biting insect that lives on animals like dogs and cats*

It seemed fairly **bothersome**: *annoying; troublesome*

I still have the **scars**: *marks that remain after cuts or scratches heal*

My friendships have **sprung from** a shared interest: *grown out of; resulted from*

I have a particular work **ethic**: *a sense of what is right and wrong; rules of behavior* [here, with respect to one's job]

a course in **linguistics**: *the study of language*

I was so **intimidated** by her coolness: *made to feel afraid or shy*

intimidated by her **coolness**: *quality of being "cool"; good; attractive* [informal]

At some point, she **revealed** to me: *told something that had been kept secret*

Neither of us was **that cool** after all: *as cool as we had thought before*

## 2 Retelling 🅛 🅢

One way to make certain that you have understood what you have heard is to retell the information to the speaker or to another listener. You do not need to use the same words.

**A** Read the following general questions before you listen to Part 1 of the interview.

  **1.** How did Catherine meet the interviewer? and how did they become friends?

  **2.** How does Catherine feel about her job, and how does that relate to her friendships?

  **3.** How did Catherine and Odette meet, and how did they get to be friends?

**B** Now listen to Part 1 of the interview with Catherine.

**C** Work with two other students. Each of you will answer one of the questions in Step A by reconstructing part of what Catherine said.

**INTERVIEW PART 2**  Maintaining Friendships

## 1 Examining vocabulary in context 🅥

Here are some words and expressions from Part 2 of the interview with Catherine, printed in **bold** and given in the context in which you will hear them. They are followed by definitions. Note: You may have already heard some of these expressions used in different contexts.

friendships need **tending**: *care; attention*

**being current** with my friends: *being up to date; knowing what is happening right now*

friends I have **managed to** stay very close to: *succeeded by making a great effort*

**snail mail**: *sending physical letters by post; non-electronic communication*

It's a **concrete** record of what we were doing: *real; physical*

did**n't** know each other **all that well**: *not very well*

**Skype**: *an Internet telephone and video service* [also: **to skype**]

show me her **knitting**: *something handmade with yarn, like a sweater or scarf*

his dog Peanut will **wander through**: *walk slowly into and out of the room, usually for no obvious reason*

it's like I've just **dropped in on** them for a visit: *paid a casual (often unexpected) visit*

There is something special about getting a letter.

## 2 Retelling Ⓛ Ⓢ

**A** Read the following general instructions before you listen to Part 2 of the interview.

**1.** Recount the story of Catherine and Doug's friendship.

**2.** Describe how Catherine uses Skype.

**B** Now listen to Part 2 of the interview with Catherine.

**C** Work with a partner. Each of you will follow one of the instructions in Step A by reconstructing part of what Catherine said.

**INTERVIEW PART 3** What Friends Do for Each Other

## 1 Examining vocabulary in context Ⓥ

Here are some words and expressions from Part 3 of the interview with Catherine, printed in **bold** and given in the context in which you will hear them. They are followed by definitions.

I want my friends to **call me on things** [that upset them]: *be honest with [me] when they are upset or angry about something [I] did or said*

Friendship can get **prickly**: *difficult; uncomfortable*

**all you have to do is** say one word: *it's very easy; you only need to . . .*

The other person can **go off into peals of laughter**: *start laughing loudly, uncontrollably*

You've actually **accrued** this common history: *built up; collected over time*

My friendships have kind of **shifted** since my son was born: *changed in a natural way as a result of changes in one's situation*

Being a parent is so **all-consuming**: *requiring all of one's energy and focus*

It really **bonds** you with people: *creates a strong interpersonal connection*

## 2 Summarizing what you have heard Ⓝ Ⓛ Ⓢ

**A** Read the following incomplete summary of Part 3 of the interview. Try to predict how you might fill in the blanks.

According to Catherine, one of the most important things that friends can do for each

other is _____ . She believes that fighting is a way to show _____ . Other

important things that friends give one another are comfort, _____ , _____ ,

and jokes.

Catherine's more recent friendships revolve around her _____ ; she thinks

that being a parent is such an _____ experience that it _____ to people who

are going through the same thing. However, she still maintains her old friendships,

thanks to e-mail, _____ , and _____ .

Finally, Catherine says that _____ are "the family _____ ."

🔊 **B** As you listen to Catherine, complete the summary by filling in the blanks. Listen again if you need to.

**C** Compare summaries with a partner. Your answers do not have to be exactly the same.

# 3 Listening for verb tense and aspect ⓛ ⓢ

> When you are listening to a narrative, you need to ask yourself, "When did this happen? Did it happen once or several times? Did it happen at one moment or did it continue over a period of time? Is it still happening?" Listening for verb *tense* (past, present, or future) and *aspect* (simple, perfect, or progressive) in English is as important to comprehension as understanding what the words mean.

🔊 **A** Listen to the excerpts from the interview with Catherine. Pay attention to the form of the verbs in each excerpt. Then circle the letter of the item that accurately completes the sentence and expresses the meaning of the excerpt.

**1.** Catherine ___ .
   a. started studying linguistics when she met Odette
   b. met Odette while she was studying linguistics
   c. met Odette before she studied linguistics

**2.** Odette said to Catherine, "___ ."
   a. I think you are much cooler than me
   b. You were much cooler than me
   c. I thought you were much cooler than me

**3.** Catherine and Doug ___ .
   a. write letters to each other
   b. started writing letters to each other more than 20 years ago
   c. both a and b

**4.** Misayo and Catherine ___ .
   a. sometimes show each other what they are knitting
   b. are planning to show each other what they are knitting
   c. both a and b

**5.** Catherine ___ .
   a. used to feel that it was OK for friends to fight
   b. now feels that it's OK for friends to fight
   c. has always felt that it's OK for friends to fight

**B** Compare your completions in a small group and then as a class. Do you agree? Listen again if you need to.

## 1 Drawing inferences Ⓢ

Work with a partner. Go back to the task Recalling what you already know (in Before the Interview, page 129) and imagine how Catherine would complete the statements.

## 2 Sharing your personal and cultural perspective Ⓢ

Discuss these questions in a small group.

1. Many of Catherine's strongest friendships are long-distance ones. Do you have any successful long-distance friendships? How often do you communicate with each other? Have the friendships changed at all?

2. Catherine believes that it is OK for friends to disagree with each other and to get angry with each other. In her view, this shows that they care about each other. What do you think? Is it acceptable in your culture for friends who care for each other to express anger openly?

3. Catherine has both male and female friends. Do you have close friends of the opposite sex? If so, how are those friendships different from your same-sex friendships? Are different-sex friendships common in your culture?

# 3 In Your Own Voice

In this section, you will tell a classmate about what you do (and used to do) with your friends.

## 1 Describing a typical scene and activities

> Part of friendly conversation involves entertaining our friends by describing typical scenes from our lives – for example, things that we enjoy doing or recurring situations that are humorous. If these are routines that will occur again in the future, we often use the **simple future tense** (*On Saturdays, we*'ll *sometimes* **go** *for a walk in the park.*) and **future progressive tense** (*Usually, the sun* **will be shining**, *and kids* **will be running** *around in the grass.*) to describe them. These tenses give listeners the sense that they can actually see the scene and experience what we are describing.

**A** You are going to tell a partner about what you typically do with a friend or group of friends. First, listen again to Catherine's description of Skyping with her friend Corey. The box contains some of the expressions she uses.

We**'ll be talking** and Corey**'ll** say something like, "**. . .**"
. . . his wife **will walk** through
. . . She**'ll stop** and **show me** her knitting
. . . and I'll **show** her what I'm working on
. . . **then the dog will wander** through

**B** Now think of some activities that you typically do with your friends. It could be playing sports, working out in a gym, going out to a café or bar, shopping, cooking, studying, making music, or anything else you and your friends routinely do together. Here is an example (playing sports) with some expressions you can use.

Using Skype to stay in touch

Playing rugby

> When the weather is nice in the spring, my friends and I like to play
> _____ .
> **We**'ll go **to the park and there**'ll be **a lot of people** talking **and** having **picnics.**
> **We**'ll start **playing, and pretty soon, a lot of other people** will join **the game.**
> **My friend** _____ will usually show up **late, and he**'ll bring **his cousin**
> _____ **with him.**
> **Then someone** will say, **"Let's** _____ !"
> **After a while, we**'ll get tired, **and we**'ll stop **playing.**
> **Sometimes, it**'ll start **to rain, and we**'ll go **and** find **a café.**
> **There**'ll be **a lot of young people. Someone** will be telling **stories about**
> _____ .
> **My friends** _____ **and** _____ will be arguing **about politics or**
> **movies.**

**C** Now talk to your partner. Tell him/her about something you enjoy doing with your
friends. Use the language in the box to describe the scene.

## 2 Reminiscing about a typical scene and activities

> When we *reminisce* (recall happy events or situations from our earlier lives that will
> probably not occur again), we can use the same language as in the first activity – all
> we need to change is **will → would**. For example:
>
> The summer when I was 10 years old, my friend _____ and I **would play**
> all day on Saturday. We'd go to the beach, and a lot of other kids **would** already **be**
> **swimming** and **playing** games, and **we would** _____ .

Tell your partner about something you used to enjoy doing with your friends.

# 4 Academic Listening and Note Taking

In this section, you will hear and take notes on a two-part lecture given by Kenneth Warden, a psychotherapist who works with individuals, couples, and families. The title of the lecture is "Looking at Friendship." Mr. Warden will talk about what friendship means to him as an individual and as a psychotherapist, and about some recent challenges to friendship.

## BEFORE THE LECTURE

## 1 Building background knowledge on the topic: Culture notes Ⓥ Ⓢ

**A** Read the following paragraph. Look up or discuss any words or expressions that are unfamiliar.

> In his lecture, Mr. Warden will refer to a popular song written by Jule Styne and performed by the American singer and actress Barbra Streisand. The song is "People." Some of the lyrics are: *People who need people are the luckiest people in the world. We're children, needing other children, and yet letting our grown-up pride hide all the need inside.*

**B** Answer these questions with a partner.

1. Explain the lyrics in your own words.
2. Do you agree with the writer of the song that it is good to need other people? Why or why not?
3. What do you think this popular song might have to do with the topic of friendship for a psychotherapist?

## 2 Building background knowledge on the topic: Statistics on friendship Ⓥ Ⓢ

**A** Read the items and look up or discuss any words that are unfamiliar.

### Online News

Top Stories    Health  |  Sports  |  Arts  |  Science     Search

- A 2006 study of female nurses with breast cancer found that those who did not have close friends were four times more likely to die from the disease as women who had 10 or more friends. Having a spouse did not make a difference.
- In Sweden, a six-year study of middle-aged men found that *lack of social support* (i.e., friends) was the second most important risk factor for heart attack and coronary heart disease. Having a spouse did not make a difference.
- A survey of people living in London found that two-thirds felt that they were losing contact with their closest friends.
- A survey of Americans found that the average person has only two close friends and 25 percent have no close friends.

**B** With a small group, restate each of the four items in your own words. Did any of these findings surprise you?

## 3 Forming generalizations Ⓢ

> When we make generalizations, they are usually based on some specific information that we have analyzed. Generalizations help us to make sense of our world. However, because every generalization has exceptions (i.e., cases that do not fit the general rule), it is a good idea to begin with some form of hedge (see page 54) when making a generalization. For example:
>
> In general, . . .
> Based on what I have read, I would conclude that . . .
> I believe one can say that . . .
> If I were to generalize, I would say . . .
> In my experience, . . .
> The studies that I have read seem to indicate that . . .

**A** In your small group, make a general statement that can be concluded from the first two items in the box in the previous activity (2A). Share your statements as a class. Did you reach similar conclusions? Discuss your differences.

**B** Now make a general statement based on the last two items in the box. Share your statements as a class. Did you reach similar conclusions? Discuss your differences.

## 4 Using morphology, context, and nonverbal cues to guess meaning Ⓝ Ⓥ Ⓛ Ⓢ

> What should you do when a lecturer uses a term that you do not know? If it seems important, write it down. You can look it up in a dictionary or ask a classmate what it means after class. In the meantime, you may be able to use *morphology*, *spoken context*, and/or *nonverbal cues* to get at least a partial sense of its meaning.
> **Morphology.** Using morphology means dividing a word up and looking for parts that you already know. If the lecturer uses a word like *indivisibility*, don't panic! You know that *in-* means "not," and *-ibility* is related to *ability*, or something being possible. *Divisi-* might remind you of other words in the same family, such as *division* and *divide.* So you see, you have enough information to figure out what *indivisibility* means.
> **Spoken context.** As with written context, spoken context will frequently help you with examples, definitions, or paraphrases of the unfamiliar vocabulary. Most lecturers repeat and explain themselves, especially when they are making an important point.
> **Nonverbal cues.** Nonverbal cues can give you at least a partial sense of an unfamiliar term. If a speaker stretches out her arms when using the word *gigantic*, for example, you can easily guess that it means "very big." Or the lecturer may use a particular tone of voice to underscore a word or phrase.

As you listen to a lecture, a partial understanding of an unfamiliar term will often be enough for your purposes. Remember, it is the whole of the lecture that you need to understand, not each of the individual words.

**A** The following terms are used in the lecture. Try to find morphological clues to their meanings.

1. **subjective:** _____

2. **social network, or support systems:** _____

3. **loners:** _____

4. **vulnerable:** _____

5. **overscheduled:** _____

**B** Now watch or listen to the lecture excerpts. As you listen, spoken context and nonverbal cues will give you more information about the meanings of these terms. Write down what you think each term means.

**C** Compare notes with a partner and then as a class. Explain how you arrived at your answers.

**LECTURE PART 1**    The Role of Friendship in Good Mental Health

# 1 Guessing vocabulary from context Ⓥ Ⓢ

**A** The following items contain some important vocabulary from Part 1 of the lecture. Each of the terms is printed in **bold** and shown in the context in which you will hear it. Work with a partner. Using context, take turns trying to guess the meanings. Note that some of these words may have different meanings in other contexts.

___ **1.** Friendship seems like a very **straightforward** topic.

___ **2.** My first memory of consciously **contemplating** friendship was as a young boy.

___ **3.** This is an important **indicator** of a person's general functioning.

___ **4.** when I work with a client who's **suicidal**

___ **5.** Suicide is very often the **manifestation** of an abject sense of alienation.

___ **6.** an **abject** sense of alienation

___ **7.** important to **hook** them **up with** their support systems so that they can be monitored

___ **8.** so that they can be **monitored** and kept safe

___ **9.** adults who consider themselves loners and say they are **content** with that

___ **10.** My sense is that it's almost always the function of a **defense mechanism**.

___ **11.** There can be a lot of pain involved with friendship; it's a **risky business**.

___ **12.** When we try to make friends, we become vulnerable to **rejection**.

___ **13.** a painful childhood memory of being **cast aside** by one friend

**B** Match the terms in Step A with their definitions by writing the letters in the blanks.

**a.** way to protect oneself, psychologically

**b.** happy; satisfied

**c.** simple; easy

**d.** thinking about killing oneself

**e.** cut off socially; abandoned; forgotten

**f.** thinking about

**g.** miserable; very bad

**h.** sign; demonstration

**i.** connect with; put in contact with

**j.** being told no by another person; offering something and having it refused

**k.** watched closely; observed frequently

**l.** something that may involve danger

**m.** sign that points to a certain conclusion

Rejection by friends is especially painful for children.

# 2 Listening for specific information 🅛 🅝 🅢

**A** Read over these questions on Part 1 of the lecture. Think about what kind of information you will need in order to answer them.

**1.** What first started the lecturer thinking about the importance of friendship? Explain.

**2.** Why is the lecturer so concerned with his clients' social networks?

**3.** When a client is considering suicide, what are the two reasons why Warden looks into the client's support system?

**4.** Why is friendship risky?

**5.** Why do some people become loners?

**B** Now watch or listen to Part 1 of the lecture. Take notes on your own paper. Use the questions in Step A as a guide to help you listen for the important points.

**C** Work with a partner. Use your notes to answer the questions in Step A. Answer as fully as you can. Then write your answers. Share them as a class.

**LECTURE PART 2**   New Challenges to Friendship

# 1 Guessing vocabulary from context Ⓥ Ⓢ

**A** The following items contain some important vocabulary from Part 2 of the lecture. Each of the terms is printed in **bold** and shown in the context in which you will hear it. Work with a partner. Using context, take turns trying to guess the meanings. Note that some of these words may have different meanings in other contexts.

    ____ **1.** There's been a lot of study recently of how **contemporary** life affects children.

    ____ **2.** Activities are good, but children also need **unstructured** time.

    ____ **3.** They can just "hang out" with their peers – without tasks or **deadlines**.

    ____ **4.** Ask a friend today "How are you?" and **odds are** the answer will be, "I'm so tired!"

    ____ **5.** the impact that social networking has had on how people **conduct** their **friendships**

    ____ **6. Facebook, instant messaging, texting, Twitter**

    ____ **7.** Friendships used to rely on face-to-face **interaction**.

    ____ **8.** And in the past it would probably have **spelled** the end of the friendship.

    ____ **9.** They can be **vital** to sustaining an existing friendship.

    ____ **10. sustaining** an existing friendship

    ____ **11.** Networking is a relatively recent **phenomenon**.

    ____ **12. It is safe to assume** that friendship will survive.

**B** Match the vocabulary terms in Step A with their definitions by writing the letters in the blanks.

**a.** there is enough evidence to conclude

**b.** modern-day; happening now

**c.** resulted in

**d.** keeping alive and healthy

**e.** have contact with friends

**f.** dates by which something must be completed (e.g., a homework assignment)

**g.** direct communication, usually between two people

**h.** necessary

**i.** an interesting event or pattern (occurring, e.g., in nature or in society) that people notice

**j.** probably; most likely

**k.** free; without rules or controls

**l.** examples of social-networking tools

# 2 Listening for specific information ⓛ ⓝ ⓢ

**A** Read over these questions on Part 2 of the lecture. Think about what kind of information you will need in order to answer them.

**1.** According to the lecturer, what contemporary challenge to friendship do children face?

**2.** What is the challenge to friendship that adults face today?

**3.** What effect has social networking had on friendships, according to Warden?

**4.** How is "social connectivity" different from friendship?

**B** Now watch or listen to Part 2 of the lecture. Take notes on your own paper. Use the questions in Step A as a guide to help you listen for the important points.

**C** Work with a partner. Use your notes to answer the questions in Step A. Answer as fully as you can. Then write your answers. Share them as a class.

A contemporary view of friendship?

# 1 Sharing your personal perspective Ⓢ

Discuss the following questions with one or two classmates.

1. The lecturer says that rejection by friends is especially painful for children. Why do you think this is so? Do you remember ever feeling left out or cast aside by friends when you were a child? Do you remember any children who didn't have friends?

2. Do you agree with the lecturer that friendship can be a "risky business"?

3. The lecturer is concerned that children do not have enough free time to develop true friendships. Do you agree or disagree? How did your early friendships develop?

4. Do you use any of the social networking tools mentioned in the lecture? If so, share what you like and don't like about them.

5. Were there any points in the lecture that you did not understand or did not agree with? If so, discuss them together.

# 2 Considering related information Ⓢ Ⓥ

Read these quotations about friendship. Then discuss the questions in a small group.

> It is not so much our friends' help that we need as the confident knowledge that they will help us. – *Epicurus*
>
> True friendship is never serene. – *Madame de Sévigné*
>
> The only way to have a friend is to be one. – *Ralph Waldo Emerson*
>
> Friendship is born at that moment when one person says to another, "What, you too? I thought I was the only one." – *C. S. Lewis*

**it is not so much [X] as [Y]** = [Y] is the important thing; [X] is not.

**serene** = calm, peaceful

1. Restate what Epicurus said in your own words. Do you agree with this statement? Explain.

2. Do you agree with Madame de Sévigné? Do you think that Catherine (see page 129) would agree?

3. Restate the Emerson quotation in your own words. Discuss what is involved in "being a friend," in your opinion.

4. Do you have any friendships that began in the way that C. S. Lewis describes? What did you have in common with these friends?

# Chapter 8
# Love

*Romeo and Juliet* – painting by Karl Ludwig Friedrich Becker

Look at the painting and answer the questions with a partner.

    **1.** What is their story?

    **2.** Why do you think their story is so famous?

## 1 Getting Started

The title of this chapter is "Love" – specifically romantic love between two people. In this section, you will read and talk about what makes two people fall in love, and what makes love last, and you will play matchmaker for six single people.

### 1 Reading and thinking about the topic Ⓥ Ⓢ

**A** Read the following passage:

What makes two people fall in love? What makes love last? These are two very different questions. It is often said that "opposites attract," and in some respects this is true. A lot of couples have certain personality differences that *complement* one another. For example, he might be shy, and she might be outgoing. However, research shows that love relationships are more likely to last if two people "*match*" each other – that is, if they have similar backgrounds, values, opinions, and interests. This makes good sense, if we think about it. Two people with similar backgrounds are more likely to understand each other and to agree on the wide range of issues that we face in long-term relationships – everything from how to raise children to what kind of car to buy.

**B** Answer the following questions according to the information in the passage:

  **1.** How would you answer the two questions at the beginning of this passage?

  **2.** What is one way in which two people might complement each other?

  **3.** In what ways do most successful couples match, according to research?

**C** Discuss your own experiences and opinions with a partner.

  **1.** Think of a married couple that you know – for example, your parents. In what ways are they similar to each other?

  **2.** In what ways are the same two people different? Do you think these differences have a positive or negative effect on the relationship?

## 2 Personalizing the topic ⓢ ⓥ

**A** Work alone. Imagine that you have gone to a matchmaking Web site that will help you find a mate. Think about what kind of person you are and what kind of mate you want.

**B** Read all the characteristics in the box. Look up any words that you do not know. Then check (✓) all the characteristics that apply to you. Add another term that applies to you in each blank.

| I am . . . | | I enjoy . . . | |
|---|---|---|---|
| shy | sensitive | _____ music | going to movies |
| serious | mature | jazz | art |
| outgoing | responsible | classical music | camping |
| athletic | easygoing | playing sports | hiking |
| fun loving | _____ | watching sports | shopping |
| adventurous | _____ | reading | _____ |
| hard working | _____ | cooking | _____ |

**C** Now think about what characteristics you are looking for in a mate. Check all the terms that apply. Add another term in each blank.

| I'd like someone who is . . . | | I'd like someone who enjoys . . . | |
|---|---|---|---|
| shy | sensitive | _____ music | going to movies |
| serious | mature | jazz | art |
| outgoing | responsible | classical music | camping |
| athletic | easygoing | playing sports | hiking |
| fun loving | _____ | watching sports | shopping |
| adventurous | _____ | reading | _____ |
| hard working | _____ | cooking | _____ |

**D** Compare the qualities you checked for yourself with those you checked for a mate. Are you looking for someone who *matches* you or someone who *complements* you?

## 3 Listening for details Ⓛ Ⓝ Ⓢ

🔊 **A** Listen to the recording. You will hear six people who are looking for a mate give a brief description of themselves. Take notes as you listen. Write down as many details as you can.

**1.** Les: _____

_____

**2.** Michael: _____

_____

**3.** Alicia: _____

_____

**4.** Frank: _____

_____

**5.** Sara: _____

_____

**6.** Suzanne: _____

_____

**B** Compare notes with a partner. Did you write the same information?

**C** Play matchmaker. Decide which person would be happiest with whom. Discuss your reasons with your partner.

**D** As a class, compare your matches. Which matches do you think would be successful, and why?

# 2 Real-Life Voices

In this section, you will hear a married couple, Ann and Jim, talk about how they met and why their relationship is successful.

**BEFORE THE INTERVIEW**

## Sharing your cultural perspective Ⓢ Ⓝ

**A** Work with a partner from another culture, if possible. Ask questions about marriage in your partner's culture and write his/her answer. If you are from the same culture, answer the questions together.

In my partner's culture/country:

**1.** At about what age do couples meet each other? _____

**2.** Where and how do couples meet? _____

**3.** How long on average do couples wait to get married? _____

**4.** Do most couples have children? How many children? _____

**5.** What percentage of married couples get divorced? _____

**B** Discuss with your partner whether any of the information above has changed recently, and, if so, how. For example, are couples getting married earlier than they did in the past? Or perhaps later?

**INTERVIEW PART 1** Courtship

## 1 Examining vocabulary in context Ⓥ

Here are some words and expressions from Part 1 of the interview with Ann and Jim, printed in **bold** and given in the context in which you will hear them. They are followed by definitions. Note that some words may have a different meaning in other contexts.

How did you **initially** get interested in each other?: *at first; in the beginning*

attending the same little **country** church: *in a rural area; not in or near a city*

I fell **head-over-heels** in love: *very quickly and completely*

This one **stuck**: *lasted; didn't disappear*

before he actually **proposed**: *asked, "Will you marry me?"*

I was so **relieved**: *happy after a period of worrying*

Did Jim **give you any encouragement**?: *show an interest; seem to be attracted*

I wasn't very good at **showing** [my interest]: *communicating*

doing my **internship**: *period of supervised work in a hospital at the end of medical school training*

**the Peace Corps**: *an organization that sends volunteers to work in developing countries*

a rather **oblique** proposal: *indirect*

permission **to have** Ann**'s hand**: *to marry [Ann]*

**It was worth the wait**: *I am glad that I waited; I do not regret it at all.*

I feel very **fortunate**: *lucky*

## 2 Listening for specific information ⓛ ⓢ

**A** Read these questions before you listen to Part 1 of the interview.

**1.** How long have Ann and Jim been married? _____

**2.** How old were they when they first met? _____

**3.** What was Ann's first impression of Jim? _____

**4.** What was Ann worried about at first? _____

**5.** How many years was it before Jim proposed? _____

**6.** Why and how did Jim finally propose? _____

**7.** Why does Ann feel "very fortunate"? _____

**B** Now listen to Part 1 of the interview. Write short answers to the questions in Step A. Listen again if you need to.

**C** Compare answers with a partner and then as a class.

---

**INTERVIEW PART 2**   Making Marriage Work

## 1 Examining vocabulary in context ⓥ

Here are some words and expressions from Part 2 of the interview with Ann and Jim, printed in **bold** and given in the context in which you will hear them. They are followed by definitions.

It wasn't a **one-sided** kind of thing: *where one person is much stronger or more important*

Our **faith** is very important to us: *religious beliefs*

differences that **work to** your **advantage**: *help; benefit*

Ann is very **meticulous**: *careful and exact; neat*

a **phenomenal** record of our 30 years together: *amazing; surprising; wonderful*

They're all **catalogued** neatly **in albums**: *filed in books designed to hold photographs*

Jim has **alluded to** it: *mentioned indirectly*

We**'re committed to** our marriage: *want to make successful; promise to support*

experiences that have **bonded** you: *united; brought closer together emotionally*

**not necessarily the happiest** [of times]: *unhappy [expressed indirectly to be polite]*

They were **challenging** [years]: *difficult, but in a positive way*

## 2 Listening for specific information ⓛ ⓢ

**A** Read the following questions before you listen to Part 2 of the interview.

**1.** What does Jim mean when he says that his and Ann's relationship isn't one-sided?

_____

**2.** What interests and beliefs do Ann and Jim share?

_____

**3.** Jim talks about a difference between himself and Ann. What is it?

_____

**4.** What quality do both Ann and Jim mention as important to the success of their marriage?

_____

**5.** Describe the experiences that have "bonded" Ann and Jim. Were they good or bad? Explain.

_____

Shared interests are important in a marriage.

**B** Now listen to Part 2 of the interview. Write short answers to the questions in Step A. Listen again if you need to.

**C** Compare answers with a partner and then as a class.

When people are recounting exciting personal events, it is very common for them to remember related details as they speak. Often these details are digressions – that is, they go "off topic." As a listener, it is important to recognize when the speaker has left the topic, and when they come back to it. Often, they will change their tone of voice or speak more quickly when they digress – in a sense, putting the digression inside verbal parentheses (*"let me just add this one little detail before I continue with my story"*). They may then repeat an earlier phrase with stress to signal that they have returned to their story.

Do not ignore digressions because they often contain important information. But be ready to pick up the story when the speaker continues.

## 3 Listening for digressions ⓛ ⓝ ⓢ

🔊 **A** Listen again to excerpts from the interview. In each excerpt, you will hear Ann or Jim make a digression as they tell the story of how they met and fell in love. After the digression, they repeat a phrase from earlier to show that they have come back "on topic." Listen for the digression and for the repeated phrase. Write the repeated phrase.

1. _____
2. _____
3. _____
4. _____

**B** Compare what you wrote with a partner.

🔊 **C** Now listen again. As a class, identify what Ann or Jim did to show that they were digressing in each excerpt. Did they speed up? Did they use different stress?

---

**AFTER THE INTERVIEW**

## 1 Sharing your personal and cultural perspective ⓢ

Discuss the following questions in a group with classmates of both sexes if possible.

1. Ann says that Jim gave her *very little* encouragement during the 11 years before they got married. Why do you think this was the case?
2. Would it be common for a woman in your culture to wait 11 years to marry the man she loved? Would a man wait that long for a woman?
3. In what ways is the marriage of Ann and Jim different from the typical successful marriage in your culture? In what ways is it similar?
4. What experiences do you think bond a couple? Name as many as you can.

## 2 Considering related information ⓢ ⓝ

**A** Here are 10 features of personal appearance that people might notice when they first meet someone. Try to predict whether men or women would be more likely to notice each feature in someone of the opposite sex. Write M next to features that you think men would notice, and write W next to those that you think women would notice.

| | | | |
|---|---|---|---|
| ___ clothing | ___ eyes | ___ figure/body | ___ face |
| ___ smile | ___ hair | ___ teeth | ___ height |
| ___ hands | ___ legs | | |

**B** The following information was taken from a study that asked men and women: "When you meet someone of the opposite sex, which one or two things about physical appearance do you tend to notice first?" One of you should look *only* at Table A, and the other *only* at Table B. Ask your partner questions to fill in the blanks in your table.

A

| Percent of Males | Percent of Females | Who first notice: |
|---|---|---|
| 29 | — | clothing |
| — | 30 | eyes |
| 45 | — | figure/body |
| — | 27 | face |
| 24 | — | smile |
| — | 16 | hair |
| 11 | — | teeth |
| — | 8 | height |
| 1 | — | hands |
| — | <0.5 | legs |

**Student A**
*What percentage of women first notice clothing?*

---

**Student B**
*What percentage of men first notice clothing?*

B

| Percent of Males | Percent of Females | Who first notice: |
|---|---|---|
| — | 35 | clothing |
| 22 | — | eyes |
| — | 29 | figure/body |
| 34 | — | face |
| — | 27 | smile |
| 16 | — | hair |
| — | 5 | teeth |
| 8 | — | height |
| — | 2 | hands |
| 6 | — | legs |

**C** As a class, make comparative statements about men and women in the United States based on information in the boxes.

> *When first meeting someone of the opposite sex, men are twice as likely as women to notice teeth.*

**D** What do *you* notice first? Take a survey in your class and compile the results on the board. Do male and female students answer differently?

# 3 In Your Own Voice

In this section, you will conduct a survey on a topic related to love, and you will interview a married couple.

## 1 Conducting a survey using the Likert scale

> The Likert scale, sometimes called the 5-point scale, is an effective, objective way to determine people's opinions on a topic. It is more accurate than the "yes-no" format because it allows for five possible responses rather than just two. The questioner reads a statement and asks for one of five responses:
> Strongly disagree
> Disagree
> Neither agree nor disagree
> Agree
> Strongly agree
> Because the responses are numeric, they can be easily compiled and interpreted.

**A** Think of a topic related to love or marriage that interests you. Some possible topics are: love marriages versus arranged marriages, the importance of personality versus physical appearance, matching versus complementing, and the best age to get married. Look back at Personalizing the topic, Step B, page 144, and Sharing your cultural perspective, Step A, page 146, for more ideas.

**B** Write two or three statements related to your topic. For example:

*Love marriages are happier than arranged marriages.*
*Personality is more important to men than physical attractiveness.*

**C** Read your statements to at least 20 people. Ask them to give their personal opinion about the statement on a scale of 1 to 5 – from *strongly disagree* (1) to *strongly agree* (5). You can include people in and outside of your class. Record their answers along with their gender, nationality, approximate age, and marital status. You may use the chart on the following page to record the answers to your survey.

| | Statement 1: | | | | | | | |
|---|---|---|---|---|---|---|---|---|
| | Statement 2: | | | | | | | |
| | Statement 3: | | | | | | | |

| | Response | | | M/F | Nation-ality | Approx. Age | Marital Status | KEYS |
|---|---|---|---|---|---|---|---|---|
| | 1 | 2 | 3 | | | | | |
| 1 | | | | | | | | Scale: |
| 2 | | | | | | | | 1 = strongly disagree |
| 3 | | | | | | | | 2 = disagree<br>3 = neither agree nor disagree |
| 4 | | | | | | | | 4 = agree |
| 5 | | | | | | | | 5 = strongly agree |
| 6 | | | | | | | | |
| 7 | | | | | | | | Marital status: |
| 8 | | | | | | | | S = single |
| 9 | | | | | | | | M = married<br>D = divorced |
| 10 | | | | | | | | W = widowed (spouse has died) |
| 11 | | | | | | | | |
| 12 | | | | | | | | |
| 13 | | | | | | | | |
| 14 | | | | | | | | |
| 15 | | | | | | | | |
| 16 | | | | | | | | |
| 17 | | | | | | | | |
| 18 | | | | | | | | |
| 19 | | | | | | | | |
| 20 | | | | | | | | |

**D** Analyze your data. Add up people's responses and look for different trends among people of different genders, nationalities, and so on. Express your results in percentages and share them as a class. For example:

*All of the men that I surveyed strongly agreed that a husband should be taller than his wife. Only 20% of the women I surveyed strongly agreed. 60% of the women had no opinion (neither agreed nor disagreed).*

## 2 Conducting an interview ⓢ Ⓝ

You are going to interview a married couple about their relationship. Choose a couple outside of your class and prepare your questions first. You can use the same kinds of questions that you heard in the interview with Ann and Jim. Think of some questions of your own as well.

*How did you get interested in each other?*
*What interests do you share?*
*How do you complement each other?*

## 3 Showing interest Ⓛ Ⓢ

When you are listening to a person tell a story, you can encourage them to feel more comfortable and to give more detail by showing an interest in what they are saying. Part of showing interest is nonverbal:

- eye contact
- facial expression
- tone of voice
- body posture

You can also show interest verbally:

- by using expressions like "Really?" "That is so funny!" "Then what happened?"
- by repeating what the speaker said
- by completing the speaker's thought if she is searching for a word

🔊 **A** Listen again to part of the interview with Ann and Jim. Notice how the interviewer shows interest. The box contains the expressions she uses.

Ann: . . . 33 years . . .
Interviewer: **Hmm. And that's a long time!**
Ann: I had to wait eleven years . . .
Interviewer: **Yeah!**
Ann: I feel very fortunate that I, that I –
Interviewer: **Yeah! That you waited.**
Ann: We share a lot of interests . . .
Interviewer: **What interests, for example?**
Ann: I remember somewhere thinking that maybe six [children] would be nice.
Interviewer: **Six!**

**B** Interview the married couple. Encourage them to tell stories to support their answers. As they talk, record them or take brief notes.

**C** In a small group, share some interesting details of your interview. Ask your classmates about their interviews.

# 4 Academic Listening and Note Taking

In this section, you will hear and take notes on a two-part lecture given by Dr. Robert Atkins, a professor of psychology. The title of the lecture is "Love: What's It All About?" Professor Atkins will explore various factors that influence people in their choice of a mate.

## BEFORE THE LECTURE

## 1 Building background knowledge on the topic Ⓥ Ⓢ

**A** You have just read that the lecture will discuss some of the different factors that influence people when they are choosing a mate. Look over the list of factors that Professor Atkins plans to cover in his lecture.

> ### Week 9: Lecture: Love: What's It All About?
>
> - The matching hypothesis – possible areas of similarity
> - Complementarity
> - The "Romeo and Juliet effect"

**B** Discuss the following questions with a partner:

1. What do you think Professor Atkins means by "the matching hypothesis"?

2. What are some areas of similarity between partners that Professor Atkins might mention?

3. You have seen the verb *to complement* earlier in this chapter. Explain what it means. What do you think the noun *complementarity* means?

4. Do you know the story of the young lovers Romeo and Juliet, from the play by William Shakespeare? Summarize the story briefly with your partner. How does the story end?

5. If the "Romeo and Juliet effect" is an explanation for why some people fall in love, what do you think it means?

## 2 Taking advantage of rhetorical questions Ⓝ Ⓛ Ⓢ

> You will find that many American lecturers like to ask questions of their students as a way to keep them interested. In the United States, students are encouraged to participate and express opinions, sometimes even in a lecture setting. You may not feel comfortable doing this at first; it may be culturally unfamiliar as well as linguistically challenging. Do not feel that you must speak.
>
> However, you may find that these questions can help you in two ways. First, the lecturer will usually pause after asking them, thus slowing down the pace of the lecture a little bit and giving you time to catch up. Second, these questions are often asked in such a way that you can predict the answers to some extent. In this sense, many are not questions at all but simply a way for the lecturer to get students to demonstrate their understanding of a point. When a lecturer asks, "Do you think that this kind of marriage will succeed?" this may really mean "In my opinion, this marriage will not succeed." Such questions are called *rhetorical questions.*
>
> Rhetorical questions can also give you clues about what is coming next. For example, after giving some specific examples to support a point, a lecturer may look up and ask something like, "Uh, okay, what else?" From this question you can guess that at least one more example or point is coming. If the lecturer asks, "What would be some similarities that we'd expect to see?" you can guess that he or she will give some examples of similarities.

 **A** Watch or listen to six rhetorical questions excerpted from the lecture. After each excerpt, analyze the purpose of the question. Is the lecturer in fact expressing an opinion? If so, in the table below place a check (✓) in the **Opinion** column. Then make a note of what you think his opinion is. Or is the lecturer asking for information? If so, check the **Asking for Information** column. Then, with a partner, recall the questions in your own words and compare your analyses. The words in the first column will help you remember the rhetorical questions.

| Excerpt | Opinion – Notes | Asking for Information |
|---|---|---|
| 1. fall in love | | |
| 2. attractiveness / a "ten" vs. a "five" | | |
| 3. education level | | |
| 4. same age | | |
| 5. opposites attract | | |
| 6. Romeo & Juliet | | |

 **B** Now watch or listen to the rhetorical questions again. This time, you will hear what follows. How accurate were you in your predictions?

# 1 Guessing vocabulary from context ⓥⓢ

**A** The following items contain some important vocabulary from Part 1 of the lecture. Each of the terms is shown in **bold** in the context in which you will hear it. Work with a partner. Using context, take turns guessing the meanings.

___ **1.** The **sociobiology** people would tend to say you fall in love unconsciously.

___ **2.** fall in love **unconsciously**

___ **3.** Guys that are tall and muscular would produce a good **gene pool**.

___ **4. homogeneity**, or similarity

___ **5.** Some people call this the **matching hypothesis**, that we tend to be attracted by somebody who is like us.

___ **6.** You're **apt to** stay married if you marry someone that's like you are.

___ **7.** Maybe she's a "**ten**," and he's a "three."

___ **8.** if she graduated from graduate school, and he **flunked out of** kindergarten

___ **9.** and he flunked out of **kindergarten**

___**10.** He kept **bugging** her about her being a college graduate.

___**11.** She didn't want to have even more of a **gap**.

___**12.** similar . . . **socioeconomic status**, age, education, things like that

**B** Match each vocabulary term in Step A with its definition below. Write the letter. Note that the definitions reflect the context in which the terms are used in the lecture.

**a.** a person's level in society and degree of wealth

**b.** distance between two people (negative connotation)

**c.** failed; did not continue in school

**d.** study of the relationship between nature and society

**e.** extremely attractive physically (on a scale of 1 to 10)

**f.** year of preschool, before elementary school

**g.** source of hereditary traits; DNA

Why do you fall in love with one person – but not another person?

**h.** sameness

**i.** theory that similar people make the best mates

**j.** complaining to

**k.** are likely to; will probably

**l.** without planning to or being aware of it; not intentionally

## 2 Outlining practice ⓃⓁⓈ

**A** Look at the following general outline of Part 1 of the lecture. Think about how the lecture will be organized and what information you will need to complete the outline.

| Love: What's It All About? Part 1 |
|---|
| I. the matching hypothesis = _____ |
|   A. possible areas of similarity |
|     1. physical |
|       e.g., _____ |
|     2. personality |
|     3. _____ |
|     4. _____ |
|     5. education |
|       e.g., _____ |
|     6. same interests |
|     7. _____ |
|     8. _____ |
|     9. race |
|     10. age |
|     11. _____ |

**B** Now watch or listen to Part 1 of the lecture. Take notes on your own paper.

**C** Compare notes with a partner. Help each other if you did not hear all the areas of similarity mentioned.

**D** Use your notes to complete the outline. You do not need to include everything; just fill in the blanks in the outline.

**E** Go over your outlines as a class. Remember, they do not have to be exactly the same.

## 1 Guessing vocabulary from context 🅥 🆂

**A** The following items contain some important vocabulary from Part 2 of the lecture. With a partner, take turns guessing what each **bold** term means, based on its context.

___ **1.** But you might say, "He's **Catholic** and she's **Jewish**."

___ **2.** We also want to marry someone who **validates** our ideas.

___ **3.** The idea that opposites attract, that's **complementary** theory.

___ **4. Academics** try to make big words out of little words [Note: The lecturer is going off topic here, making a joke.]

___ **5.** Difference. Well, that can work for **magnets**. [Note: Another joke.]

___ **6.** If a person is **dominant**, is he or she better off with another dominant person?

___ **7.** Is he or she **better off** with another dominant person?

___ **8.** a person that's more **submissive**, who likes people telling him or her what to do

**B** Match the terms in Step A with these definitions. Write the letter.

**a.** controlling; wanting to tell others what to do

**b.** examples of religious faiths

**c.** objects that attract metals with opposite forces

**d.** agrees with; confirms

**e.** obedient; happy to do what he or she is told

**f.** more likely to be happy or successful

**g.** professors and scholars

**h.** having differences that work together to act as advantages

## 2 Outlining practice 🅝 🅛 🆂

**A** Look at the following outline of Part 2 of the lecture. Think about how the rest of the lecture will be organized and what information you will need to complete the outline.

| Love: What's it all about? Part 2 |
| --- |
| I. (cont.) The matching hypothesis, general rule: _____ _____ |
|    *A.* possible areas of similarity (cont.) _____ |
| II. Complementarity = idea that "opposites attract" – sometimes works in rel'shps    e.g., _____ |
| III. "Romeo and Juliet effect" = _____ |
| IV. Conclusion: _____ |

**B** Now watch or listen to Part 2 of the lecture. Take notes on your own paper.

**C** Compare notes with a partner.

**D** Use your notes to complete the outline.

**E** Go over your outlines as a class. Remember, they do not have to be exactly the same.

AFTER THE LECTURE

# 1 Applying general concepts to specific data ⓢ

Read the following questions and answer them in a small group.

1. Go over the factors mentioned in the lecture. Which of these apply to the relationship between Ann and Jim? Which do not apply, in your opinion? Explain.
2. Look again at the data in the task, Considering related information in Step B, page 150. How do you think this information relates to what Professor Atkins said in his lecture? How important are first impressions? What purpose do you think they serve?

# 2 Sharing your personal and cultural perspective ⓢ

Read and think about the following questions, and then share your ideas with a small group.

1. The lecturer stated that as a general rule, people of the same religion and race have a better chance of staying married. Do you know any couples of mixed race, religion, or culture? Do you think that they face more difficulties than other couples?
2. How powerful do you think the "Romeo and Juliet effect" is? Do you know of any couples who have experienced opposition from their families? What was the result?
3. This chapter has focused on marriages in the United States and what makes them successful. It's important to remember that in the United States, about 50 percent of all first marriages end in divorce. Considering the information that you heard in the lecture, why do you think there are so many failed marriages in the United States?
4. Were there any points in the lecture that you did not understand or did not agree with? Discuss them with your classmates or your teacher.

# 3 Considering related information ⓢ ⓥ

**A** Read the following article, adapted from an online resource. It is written in an informal style, so there may be words and expressions that you do not know. Try to guess at their general sense from context. Look them up only if you need to.

# FOUR REASONS WHY PEOPLE MARRY THE **WRONG** PERSON

**1. Anticipating a personality change after the wedding.** A common mistake amid newlyweds is expecting the other person to change once the vows are taken. While most people do change for the better with time, it's unrealistic to expect instant behavior changes. If you can't stand smoking or poor hygiene, it wouldn't be wise to marry a person who possesses these habits.

**2. Marrying on the rebound.** Following a breakup, the quickest way to get over the old relationship is to find a new one. The rebound relationship has its advantages and disadvantages. The good news is that they can quickly lift a bad mood and bring a little sunshine back into your life. The bad news is that some people are so unwilling to be alone that they don't take time to heal after a breakup, and they may just end up marrying a person they barely know.

**3. Looking for happiness.** Marriage is not a cure for depression or loneliness. Many singles believe that getting married will immediately eliminate that lingering black cloud. However, if you were unhappily single, you'll probably be unhappily married. Don't rely on another person to make you happy. Before looking for a mate, work on trying to make yourself happy. Discover new interests or volunteer with an organization. If necessary, consult a therapist.

**4. Different life goals.** For a marriage to be successful, both husband and wife must be on the same page. Before marriage, couples must discuss their long-term or future goals. Do you want children? Would you like to relocate? When goals disagree, couples eventually proceed in different directions. While dating, couples should have candid discussions. If possible, reach a compromise. However, when goals clash considerably, it's time for the couple to rethink their relationship.

**B** Discuss these questions in a small group.

1. Do you believe that people get married with the idea that they can change their spouse? Have you seen this happen?

2. Have you ever known anyone who remarried very quickly after a divorce? What was the result?

3. Do you agree with the writer that getting married is not a good way to overcome loneliness? Why or why not?

4. Which theory mentioned in the lecture would the writer agree with? Which would she disagree with? Explain your answer.

# Unit 4 Academic Vocabulary Review

This section reviews the vocabulary and topics from Chapters 7 and 8. For a complete list of all the Academic Word List words in this book, see the Appendix on pages 181–182.

## 1 Word forms

Read the sentences and fill in the blanks with a form of the word. For verbs, use the correct tense and person. For nouns, use the correct number (singular or plural). Note: You will not use all of the word forms given.

1. **indicator, indication, to indicate, indicative:**

   The inability to sleep, or insomnia, is _____ of a physical or psychological problem.

   The quality of a person's friendships is a strong _____ of her mental health.

   The presence of chronic depression _____ a serious problem.

2. **opposite, opposition, to oppose:**

   The concept of complementarity – the idea that _____ attract – has some truth to it.

   Couples in love who face _____ from their parents may be more likely to get married than those whose parents approve of their relationship.

3. **maintenance, to maintain:**

   _____ friendships over long distances is not easy.

   Friendships, like houses and automobiles, require _____ .

4. **assumption, to assume:**

   It is wrong to _____ that friendships will last forever; friendships must be cultivated.

   For some users of Facebook, the idea of friending is based on the _____ that the more friends you have, the better.

5. **to hypothesize, hypothesis, hypothetical, hypothetically:**

   The matching _____ states that we are attracted to those who are like us.

   Professor Atkins _____ that two people with a very large age gap will not have a successful marriage. Atkins is speaking _____ ; he admits that there are always exceptions to the rule.

6. **to validate, validation, valid, validity:**

   We are comfortable with people who _____ our opinions. Someone who always questions the _____ of our beliefs will probably not be a good match for us.

7. **to complement, complementary, complementarity:**

   A person with a very strong need to be in control may do better with a partner who _____ him/her, rather than one with a similar personality.

   The theory of _____ may account for initial attraction, but a couple is more likely to find long-term happiness if they are alike.

8. **to dominate, dominant:**

   A _____ person may be attracted to a submissive person.

   Some people feel the need to _____ in a relationship.

## 2 Topic review

Read the questions. Each question is followed by a box containing related words and phrases from Unit 4. General academic vocabulary is given in **bold**. Answer the questions with a partner; the words and phrases in the boxes will help you to recall the answers.

## The importance of friendship

1. Discuss why friendship is important, according to the Chapter 7 lecture.

> social **network** / support system / general **functioning** / suicidal / **monitor** / **depressed**

2. What risks are involved in friendship, and why is it important to take those risks?

> repeated **rejection** / being **rejected** / vulnerable / **isolation** / **depressed**

## Challenges to friendship

3. What **challenges** to friendship do children face today, according to the lecturer?

> **concept** of overscheduled child / deadlines / **affect** / **contemporary** life / develop friendships

4. What is the role of social **networking** in **maintaining** friendships?

> **aspect** of modern life / **communication** / face-to-face **interaction** / **sustaining** friendships / **contact** with friends / Facebook / "friending"" / recent **phenomenon** / **sustaining** friendships / long-distance / Skype / **survive**

## Love

5. What is the matching **hypothesis**? Discuss whether it works in a relationship.

> **similarity** / **similar** / **validate** / unconscious / **physical** attractiveness / education / socio**economic status** / interests / age **range** / religion / values / gap

6. What is **complementary theory**? Discuss whether **complementarity** works in a relationship.

> opposites attract / **dominant** vs. submissive / **validate** / conservative vs. **liberal** / **factor**

7. What is the "Romeo and Juliet effect"? According to Dr. Atkins, does it result in successful relationships?

> opposition / **theory** / **couples** / attractive / **factor**

# Oral Presentation

In this final section, you will be preparing and giving an oral presentation with two classmates. The subject of the presentation is a famous friendship or love relationship. You may choose either people from real life (living or dead) or a fictitious relationship (e.g., from a movie, television show, cartoon, or book). You will describe how the relationship developed, and hypothesize why it is/was successful or not successful. Use the ideas on friendship and love presented in this unit to support your opinions.

## BEFORE THE PRESENTATION

## 1 Working with a group to prepare a presentation

**A** As a class, brainstorm a list of famous lovers and friends. Think of as many as you can! Write them on the board.

Romeo & Juliet

Cleopatra & Marc Antony

Bonnie & Clyde

John Lennon & Yoko Ono

Butch Cassidy & the Sundance Kid

Batman & Robin

Sherlock Holmes & Dr. Watson

Brutus & Julius Caesar

**B** Find two other students who are interested in the same topic as you. Decide how to divide up the presentation. Use the Internet or library resources to prepare your presentation.

## 2 Organizing your presentation

There are different ways to divide up the "ownership" of your presentation. Here is one possible division:

- First presenter: Introduce the topic; give background information on the two people that you will present.
- Second presenter: Recount the meeting of the two people and the course of their relationship.
- Third presenter: Analyze and evaluate the relationship with reference to the content of this unit.

# 3 Providing visual material

Prepare a visual representation of the people that you are presenting. It could be a photograph, a short video, a drawing, a PowerPoint slide, or any other media that are available to you. This is especially important if you are presenting people who are not known to your classmates (they may be well known in your country but not worldwide).

## DURING THE PRESENTATION

## Keys to a successful presentation: Providing a road map and using rhetorical questions

**Providing a road map.** It is especially important in a group presentation to provide clear directions as you change presenters. Some repetition is absolutely acceptable in this case; it will help your audience to follow the course of your presentation. Here is some language that each presenter can use:

**First presenter:** *Today [student 2], [student 3], and I will be presenting*

_____ .
*I will begin by introducing _____ .*
*[. . .]*
*Next, [student 2] will talk to you about _____ .*

**Second presenter:** *Thanks, [student 1]. OK. As [student 1] said, I'm going to*

_____ .
*[. . .]*
*Finally, [student 3] will present our analysis of _____ .*

**Third presenter:** *Thank you, [student 2]. OK, now I'm going to _____ .*
*[. . .]*

**Using rhetorical questions.** As you recall from the Chapter 8 lecture, rhetorical questions are a good way to engage your audience (see page 156). Some students may feel too shy to respond to you, but some will probably answer.

When it is your turn, go to the front of the room as a group. Sit quietly and listen with attention to your fellow presenters. When it is your turn to speak, relax. Speak slowly and loudly. Refer to your notes as you need to, but keep your focus on your audience.

## Self-evaluation

Self-evaluation, or judging the quality of your own work, can be an effective tool for identifying areas where you need to improve. It is important to identify the specific areas that you are evaluating so that you can focus on them the next time you give a presentation.

**A** When you finish your presentation, thank your classmates and group members. Then take about five minutes to evaluate how you did. Use the form below or create your own form.

| Area to Evaluate | Self-Evaluation: What was good? What can I improve? |
| --- | --- |
| My work in my group | |
| My preparation/research for the presentation | |
| My presentation:<br>– eye contact<br>– speaking pace<br>– volume | |
| – Audience comprehension / enjoyment | |

**B** After all the presentations have been given, share your self-evaluations within your group. Do they agree with you? Do you agree with their self-evaluations? Give them feedback. Be positive. Offer helpful suggestions if you have any.

# Lectures: Video Script

## Unit 1: Mind, Body, and Health
### Chapter 1: The Influence of Mind over Body

---

## Lecture:
## "Stress and the Immune System"

**Before the Lecture**
**Using telegraphic language, page 13**

1. Think of people that you know with migraine headaches or high blood pressure, skin rashes, high cholesterol, heart disease. The list goes on and on. All of these symptoms may be related to psychosomatic disorders.

2. We have found through research that the efficiency of the immune system is compromised, d- damaged, by certain stressors, and we have support for this from two areas of research – both from humans and from animals.

3. We find that today it is widely accepted in the medical field … among health care professionals, that the mind has a powerful effect on the body, and that this effect is especially negative when a patient feels helpless, when he feels he has no control

4. …. In the case of problems like headaches, uh, sleeplessness, um, even high blood pressure, more and more health care providers are teaching patients to control these by simple relaxation techniques, which can be very effective – more effective than medication.

---

## Lecture Part 1:
## "Psychoneuroimmunology (PNI) and Animal Studies on Stress"

**Summarizing what you have heard, page 15**

It seems obvious that the mind will have an effect on the body, and in recent years, we've gathered some hard data that this is true, that the way that you think actually affects the way your body feels. Um, stress has real implications, in terms of what it can do to the body, and psychosomatic disorders, or disorders where there is a physical symptom caused by a psychological problem, is a real hot topic in psychology today, um, because it's the border between psychology and medicine and relevant to almost all areas of our lives. Think of people that you know with migraine headaches or high blood pressure, skin rashes, high cholesterol, heart disease. The list goes on and on. All of these symptoms may be related to psychosomatic disorders. What I want to focus on today is an area of research on stress and illness, and this field is called psychoneuroimmunology, or PNI for abbreviation. I suggest that you abbreviate it. The word psycho neuro immunology: psycho means the mind, the way that a person thinks; neuro is the nervous system; and immunology is the body's defenses against disease, the immune system. The immune system has two important tasks: basically to recognize foreign invaders, things that come into the body, and then to inactivate them and remove them from the body. We have found through research that the efficiency of the immune system is compromised, d- damaged, by certain stressors, and we have support for this from two areas of research – both from humans and from animals. And I'll start with some of the animal studies: So, we know that rats or mice that are placed in a situation where there was uncontrollable or unpredictable stress, uh – for example, shining bright lights on them or giving them electrical shocks to their feet or overcrowding them, which, you know, would be stressful – when these rats are infected with cancer cells and then placed in an environment like that, they're much more likely to develop cancer under these stressful conditions than if they're in nonstressful conditions. Another really important study done with animals and immune functioning was done by a fellow named Robert Ader, and Ader was actually doing a study on taste aversion in rats when he discovered, quite by accident, that he was able to condition the rats' immune systems to malfunction. Now, this has very powerful implications because if we can teach the immune system, if, if we can condition it to malfunction, then it makes sense that we could also condition it to get better and to heal itself without medicine, and that's very exciting. And that's where we are now, in this research.

## Lecture Part 2:
## "Human Research on PNI"
**Summarizing what you have heard,** page 18

And some of the studies on humans also support this idea that the mind can control the immune system. We know that people under great stress – when we analyze some of their immune functioning – we know that right before they experience a stressor, their immune systems become compromised – uh, for example, accountants before tax time or students before final exams. So if you think in terms of classical conditioning, y'know, uh, like Pavlov and his experiments with dogs, in our case, the mental stress of just thinking about the exam or just thinking about being very busy at work is acting like, uh, like Pavlov's bell – acting as a conditioned stimulus to depress the immune system. We find that today it is widely accepted in the medical field … among health care professionals, that the mind has a powerful effect on the body, and that this effect is especially negative when a patient feels helpless, when he feels he has no control. Um, elderly people in nursing homes. We know that, there was one study done on nursing home residents: one group of elderly people who felt that they were in control of their lives and they made the choice to be there; another group who felt that they were placed there by their family members, and who really didn't want to be there and they felt out of the control of the decision. Well, the ones who felt out of control were much more likely to get sick and to die, to lead unhealthy lives, while the ones who felt in control tended to be healthier. And there's another way in which the mind can exert a positive influence on the body…. In the case of problems like headaches, uh, sleeplessness, um, even high blood pressure, more and more health care providers are teaching patients to control these by simple relaxation techniques, which can be very effective – more effective than medication. So, there's real exciting implications with this work and…, we're just beginning to understand how powerful the mind is in controlling the body.

## Chapter 2: Lifestyle and Health

## Lecture:
## "Risk Factors in Cardiovascular Disease"
**Before the Lecture**
**Using symbols and abbreviations,** page 35

1. By cardiovascular disease, I mean heart attacks, strokes, and peripheral vascular disease.

2. Males appear to be at a higher risk for cardiovascular disease than females.

3. Obesity technically means at least 20 percent above ideal weight. Clearly, this puts a person at increased risk for diabetes and high blood pressure.

4. What may be happening is that acute and chronic stress results in higher blood pressure and cholesterol levels, more smoking, overeating, etc. – all of which are direct risk factors for cardiovascular disease.

## Lecture Part 1:
## "Unalterable Risk Factors in CVD"
**Outlining practice,** page 38

Today I'm going to be speaking on risk factors for cardiovascular disease. By cardiovascular disease, I mean heart attacks, strokes, and peripheral vascular disease, which is also known as clots to the legs. When the arteries become diseased, there's a, a loss of elasticity so that the arteries are not as flexible as they used to be. There can also be partial or complete blocking of the arteries. When a person has a heart attack, what happens is there's a partial or complete blocking of one or more of the arteries which feed the heart muscle. In a stroke, we're talking about the blocking of one or more of the arteries which feed the brain. In peripheral vascular disease, again, also known as clots to the legs, there's a partial blockage of one or more of the arteries to usually one of the legs. Now, there are risk factors which do give us an idea of who might develop one of these problems or these diseases. Some of the risk factors are alterable. That is, that the person at risk can actually do something about them. And then there are some risk factors which are unalterable. I'm going to run through the unalterable ones first and then the alterable ones second. OK, the unalterable risk factors are number one: gender. Males appear to be at a higher risk for cardiovascular disease than females, at least up until 50 years of age. The simplest explanation is that estrogen, a hormone which is made in women's bodies up until menopause, appears to protect women from cardiovascular disease. Second, age. As a person ages, their risk of getting cardiovascular disease increases. There's not much we can do about aging, but that is a factor – that the older a person is, the higher their risk for cardiovascular disease. Third, diabetes. People with diabetes have a higher rate of cardiovascular disease. It's not known why, but unfortunately the statistics support this. And then, family history. We all have, and need to have certain amounts of fats and fatty acids that our bodies use metabolically, and as long as our cholesterol and some of these other fat-containing chemicals in the blood are kept in good, low, balanced way, they create no increased risk to a person. However, if they get to be in higher levels than is healthy, they can create a higher risk for cardiovascular disease. And this is to some extent hereditary. In fact, when you hear about youngish men, let's say men in their thirties who have heart attacks or strokes, usually it's because of family history. I mean, even if they have other risk factors, having a heart attack in one's thirties is very rare, and the cause is usually hereditary. So, those are the unalterable risk factors for cardiovascular disease.

## Lecture Part 2:
## "Alterable Risk Factors in CVD"
### Outlining practice, page 39

The alterable risk factors for cardiovascular disease include, first of all, high blood pressure. High blood pressure, again, does tend to run in families, but there are some very, very good medications that people can take that have very few side effects in order to control high blood pressure. High blood pressure often occurs in people who are obese, um, very overweight. But then there are many otherwise healthy people who simply have high blood pressure. And the important thing is to get these people on an appropriate medication, usually a combination of medications, and keep their blood pressure within a healthy range, and that will decrease their risk of cardiovascular disease. Next, obesity. A very high percentage of Americans are considered obese. Obesity technically means at least 20 percent above ideal weight. Clearly, this puts a person at increased risk for diabetes and high blood pressure, and so it's very important to get rid of that excess weight. However, if I knew how to cure obesity, I would be an extremely wealthy woman. It's a very, very complex disease process. Generally, a low-fat diet is recommended for people who are obese. Next, cigarette smoking is clearly a risk factor for cardiovascular disease. People who smoke cigarettes have more heart attacks and strokes and peripheral vascular disease, you know, blood clots in the legs. Clearly, they have a higher incidence of these diseases earlier in life, than nonsmokers. Tobacco use not only raises blood pressure, but it probably affects the way fats are metabolized as well. And then, psychosocial factors, and this would include social isolation, certain personality traits, and of course daily stress, like a high-pressure work situation; the evidence suggests that these factors put a person at increased risk for cardiovascular disease. However, more research is needed to understand how stress contributes to risk for heart disease. We're not sure whether stress directly contributes to increased risk for cardiovascular disease. What may be happening is that acute and chronic stress results in higher blood pressure and cholesterol levels, more smoking, overeating, etc., all of which are direct risk factors for cardiovascular disease. And then finally, sedentary lifestyle is the last factor to be added to the list of alterable risk factors for cardiovascular disease. People who do not exercise, even if they have low blood pressure, are not obese, do not have diabetes, are female, don't smoke cigarettes, are young, control their stress, and eat a low-fat diet, people who, even if all those factors are in their favor, if a person does not exercise, they increase their chances of cardiovascular disease. So, there we go – another good reason to exercise.

# Unit 2: Development Through Life
## Chapter 3: The Teen Years

---

### Lecture:
### "Erik Erikson's Fifth Stage of Psychosocial Development: Adolescence"

**Before the Lecture**
**Using space to show organizational structure,** page 58

I wanna mention some of the specific, more recent … challenges that adolescents face in Western culture – drugs and alcohol. There's tremendous pressure in this age group to make decisions about use of drugs and alcohol and other mind-altering substances – smoking cigarettes, and so forth. And what we know now – there's been a lot of study on this in the last several decades – is that people who start using substances that have brain effects are really at a disadvantage of … just for example, if a kid starts smoking marijuana at age 12, it stops … the emotional growth … that comes from having to deal with experience … "naked" (little laugh) – the drug acts as a protective screen between you and the reality that you're trying to learn about and come to terms with, and so for kids who use it chronically, that aspect, that line of development … just stops, so when young people who, for example, use alcohol in their teens and then some time in their twenties are able to stop using alcohol, they discover – to their shock – that they still feel like they're 15, when they started using. This effect – this limitation of brain development – is now documented, and it makes life very difficult for these kids.

Another thing that's happening now in the last few years has to do with the amount of information that is instantly available because of the Internet and iPods and iPhones, and being able to have all kinds of distractions and instant conversations and information, and there are wonderful things about it, but also, we have no idea what the impact of that is on developing brains … we have no idea. Ever since the advent of television, this has been a point of discussion, and there has been lots of research on the impact of television on the development of child and adolescent brains – and when computer games – video games – came along, – it was even more of an issue because they are hypnotizing in a way that TV is not… . They involve the brain in such a way that kids are really hypnotized by the experience. On its face, it's not a problem, but these are environmental stimuli that in the past were not available to kids in the way that they are today, so we don't know about the impact on developing brains, and on psychological development. And again, I am not saying that they're bad, simply that we don't know about their long-term effects.

---

### Lecture Part 1:
### "Adolescence: Identity versus Role Confusion"

**Organizational structure,** page 61

Ok, to review: we've been talking about psychologist Erik Erikson and his eight stages of psychosocial development, and you'll recall that each stage is expressed in terms of a conflict that ideally, the developing person resolves in order to move on to the next stage, so for example, the first stage, basic trust versus mistrust … this is a process that goes on for many years, but the establishment of basic trust happens from birth to about age two.

So moving ahead, today we're looking at stage five, roughly the adolescent period, which covers about ages 12 to 16. Erikson's terms for this stage are identity versus role confusion, and the primary work of an adolescent in the psychosocial realm is to firmly establish their individual identity. If they are unable to do this, there's a danger of what Erikson called role confusion, or not being able to make good choices or even know what your choices are when it's very important to do so. There are a few components to this work. One of the really big challenges of this period is that this is also the time of physical and genital maturation, which is terribly confusing for kids - it hardly matters what you tell them about what's gonna happen to their bodies, the experience of it and the rapidity of the physical growth is just really shocking… . You may have had the experience of not seeing someone who is 14 years old for a couple of months and when you see them again, they've grown six inches. And kids who are going through this are very, very self-absorbed … and worried about being socially accepted, so that in the midst of this physical change there is a demand socially and psychologically – by the individual and by the people around him or her – to grow up, to establish a psychological identity, ego identity, to be able to think beyond their own physical feelings and to keep hold of that basic trust that they're gonna make it through this period … and it is a really major challenge. And lots of kids hit the wall a few times before they actually feel confident and in control of their own direction, although most kids do make it through ok.

There's another, material challenge that arises in this work of establishing identity. And that…is making a choice about one's career, one's work. More and more kids successfully postpone this choice for a few years without too much worry by continuing their education. But even so, there's a surprising amount of anxiety that people have researched over the years in the area of career choice for adolescents.

And then, another big part of this work involves the whole question of falling in love…and gender identity. All of that comes way to the fore during this period, and it's important in terms of ego identity because finding someone who you can fall in love with brings up new aspects of yourself that didn't need to be touched before, and it's quite a dramatic change, and – one hopes that it's a wonderful change, but sometimes not – and in any case, very challenging.

## Lecture Part 2:
## "Identity versus Role Confusion: New Challenges"
### Organizational structure, page 63

I wanna mention some of the specific, more recent … challenges that adolescents face in Western culture – drugs and alcohol. There's tremendous pressure in this age group to make decisions about use of drugs and alcohol and other mind-altering substances – smoking cigarettes, and so forth. And what we know now –

there's been a lot of study on this in the last several decades – is that people who start using substances that have brain effects are really at a disadvantage of … just for example, if a kid starts smoking marijuana at age 12, it stops … the emotional growth … that comes from having to deal with experience … "naked" (little laugh) – the drug acts as a protective screen between you and the reality that you're trying to learn about and come to terms with, and so for kids who use it chronically, that aspect, that line of development … just stops, so when young people who, for example, use alcohol in their teens and then some time in their twenties are able to stop using alcohol, they discover – to their shock – that they still feel like they're 15, when they started using. This effect – this limitation of brain development – is now documented, and it makes life very difficult for these kids.

Another thing that's happening now in the last few years has to do with the amount of information that is instantly available because of the Internet and iPods and iPhones, and being able to have all kinds of distractions and instant conversations and information, and there are wonderful things about it, but also, we have no idea what the impact of that is on developing brains … we have no idea. Ever since the advent of television, this has been a point of discussion, and there has been lots of research on the impact of television on the development of child and adolescent brains – and when computer games – video games – came along, – it was even more of an issue because they are hypnotizing in a way that TV is not… . They involve the brain in such a way that kids are really hypnotized by the experience. On its face, it's not a problem, but these are environmental stimuli that in the past were not available to kids in the way that they are today, so we don't know about the impact on developing brains, and on psychological development. And again, I am not saying that they're bad, simply that we don't know about their long-term effects.

Another thing to realize about adolescents is that they are experiencing their first true autonomy, being able to go out on their own without adult protection all the time, and they're seeking stimulation… . It's not as if they're trying to be careful; they are trying to be stimulated. They will take risks, and they will seek stimulation until they either have a problem, or a car wreck, or come to their own realization as to what they need to focus on and what they need to do, and this is a normal, necessary process at this age, but what is different today is that there are these new ways to become involved in stimuli that may not be helpful…and could be harmful.

## Chapter 4: Adulthood

### Lecture:
### "Developmental Tasks of Early Adulthood"
**Before the Lecture**
**Paying attention to signal words, page 74**

1. By developmental tasks, I mean life changes that a person must accomplish as he or she grows and develops

2. Ideally, what's considered optimal at this point is for the young adult to be capable of supporting him- or herself completely – that includes financially, emotionally, and socially.

3. One of the major tasks for young adults is the development of a new and different type of relationship with parents – that is, one based on mutual adulthood.

4. the current economic climate in the world has made that much more difficult to achieve, and the result is that we see a lot more young adults living with their parents.

5. So, as I said, it, it can be difficult for young adult children to establish financial independence from their parents.

6. Of course, separation is the natural thing for adult children to do at this point – to leave their parents and, and start their own, uh, lives. But even though it's natural, this is still a crisis point in a family, when a child leaves

7. So, we've talked about two of the important tasks of young adulthood.

### Lecture Part 1:
### "Separation from Parents"
**Listening for specific information, page 76**

I'm going to speak about two of the major developmental tasks of young adulthood, and by developmental tasks, I mean life changes that a person must accomplish as he or she grows and develops. The young adult is in his or her early to mid-twenties, and at least in Western culture, um, this is the time for the achievement of independence from parents. Ideally, what's considered optimal at this point is for the young adult to be capable of supporting him- or herself completely – that includes financially, emotionally, and socially. [slight pause] OK, so we could say that one of the major tasks for young adults is the development of a new and different type of relationship with parents – that is, one based on mutual adulthood. Now, this is the sort of culmination of a long process of separation that starts in early childhood, and ideally in young adulthood, and the child physically separates and goes his or her own way in the world. Interestingly enough, this is a change that is happening later in, in life, in today's world, partly because it depends on the child's ability to become financially independent, and the current economic climate in the world has made that much more difficult to achieve, and the result is that we see a lot more young adults living with their parents, well, well into their twenties. So, as I said, it, it can be difficult for young adult children to establish financial independence from their parents. And then, establishing emotional independence can also be a difficult process, and not all children separate from their parents with equal success. Some children may never be successful at this, uh, they may be forever in the role of child and the parent forever in the role of parent. Of course, [slight pause] separation is the natural thing for adult children to do at this point – to leave their parents and, and start their own, uh, lives. But even though it's natural, this is still a crisis point in a family, when a child leaves, and some families don't handle it well. Change is, a frightening thing for, for many people, but there's no escaping it. We all have to learn how to change throughout our lives.

## Lecture Part 2:
## "The Crisis of Intimacy versus Isolation"
**Listening for specific information,** page 78

And then there's a second task of young adulthood, which ties – uhh – into this whole business of getting married. Erik Erikson identifies, th, the period of young adulthood as the time when the young adult faces the crisis of intimacy versus isolation. Well, the theory is that in adolescence, the child has developed a healthy uh ego identity, and of course in reality, um, for a variety of reasons, many people fail to develop this healthy identity in adolescence, but again, ideally, then, in young adulthood, this identity is ready and able to be joined with another, uh, traditionally in marriage. This involves the ability to make a commitment to someone, in, a, a close intimate way. Now, according to Erikson, healthy people during this period – umm – are able to compromise, to sacrifice, to negotiate – all of which one must do to make a marriage successful. This, then, as I said, is a second major development task, I mean, developmental task of this period. The ability to adapt to another person in this way will increase intimacy, or closeness and, and connection. Um, if this isn't achieved, the result is isolation, or in other words, a kind of avoiding of being in the world. Other people experience this as self-absorption, and we've seen, for example, um, someone who is a really accomplished research chemist, but they spend all their time in the lab, and their family is estranged. And, and, and, and this isn't a natural choice for a human being. We are built to be in groups, and people who isolate themselves often have, um, excellent reasons for doing so, but the reasons are negative … so, there is a fear of losing themselves or, or, being hurt if, if, they open up and are vulnerable to other people. So, there you have intimacy or isolation, and the challenge for the young adult is to resolve that crisis, and, as I said, success depends on the young adult having developed a healthy, a solid, healthy identity in adolescence. It's difficult to give yourself to another person in a relationship, if you do not have a self to give, if your self is not defined, if it is not solid… and, it puts great emotional stress on a relationship when two people

are trying to deal with the developmental tasks of marriage, wh – wh – when they haven't yet dealt with the important developmental task involved in just being a separate person. That, ideally, should come first. And that brings me to an interesting point about marriage today…a, and that is that increasingly, in the West, people who in the past might have felt pressure to marry in their early twenties, uh, right out of college, now tend to stay single for a longer period of time. With this is the freedom, for example, to take more risks, to move to a different part of the country or to a different part of the world. And there is also, with, what with the divorce rate as high as it is, a certain reluctance, a skepticism about marriage as an institution. As a result, many young adults are waiting to get married until their late twenties or older. And in fact, the, the statistics show that couples who do wait till their late twenties to get married have a much lower divorce rate than, than those who marry in their early twenties. So, we've talked about two of the important tasks of young adulthood: the first, separation from parents, which involves, uh, renegotiating one's, one's relationship with parents; and the second, solving the crisis of intimacy versus isolation, that is, bringing a solid sense of one's self to a relationship with another person. And, the degree of success with which the young uh adult accomplishes these tasks will determine to a great extent their future success and satisfaction in life.

## Unit 3: Nonverbal Messages
## Chapter 5: Body Language

## Lecture:
## "Body Language Across Cultures"
**Before the Lecture:**
**Mapping,** page 98

Maybe we should begin by mentioning an obvious one; that's what we call body language, that is, what we are saying by our posture, the way in which we hold ourselves, our gestures, that is, use of our hands; our facial expressions – all the things that say something to the other person, not through words, but simply how we present ourselves, how we move.

Let's see, our eye contact, for example, is one that we may not think of right away, but, it's extremely important, and our tone of voice. How about the meaning of touch? Touch communication, that is, who has permission to touch whom and under what circumstances.

## Lecture Part 1:
## "Aspects of Body Language"
**Mapping,** page 99

OK. Today we're going to begin our discussion of nonverbal communication. Now, experts in the field of communication estimate that somewhere between 60 and 90 percent of everything we communicate is nonverbal. How can that possibly be true? After all, we put so much emphasis on our words when we're trying to communicate something. We think about what we want to say, we worry about what we didn't say. We think about what we should have said. I mean, we're concerned about how the other person interprets our words, and we interpret the other person's words. So, there's enormous emphasis in all our interactions on words. What about this 60 to 90 percent that is supposedly nonverbal? What does that mean exactly? OK. Let me ask you to think about some of the ways in which you communicate nonverbally – just the broad areas. Maybe we should begin by mentioning an obvious one; that's what we call body language, that is, what we are saying by our posture, the way in which we hold ourselves, our gestures, that is, use of our hands; our facial expressions – all the things that say something to the other person, not through words, but simply how we present ourselves, how we move. Let's see, our eye contact, for example, is one that we may not think of right away, but, it's extremely important, and our tone of voice. How about the meaning of touch? Touch communication, that is, who has permission to touch whom and under what circumstances. A very important point that I'd like to make is that nonverbal communication is difficult enough to study and understand in one's own culture, but – it becomes extremely complicated when we are trying to understand how nonverbal communication functions

in another culture, that is, one we're unfamiliar with. I mean, after all, if we're learning about another culture and learning the language of that culture, another language, what do we learn but words – the meaning of words and how they fit together and the pronunciation of words. So that, when we learn French, we can take our dictionary and look up fromage, or when we learn German, we can find out what Käse is. But, there's no dictionary of nonverbal communication. So, where do we find out what a certain toss of a head means? Or a certain blink of the eye? Or the physical distance between people? It's very easy to misinterpret these cues or to miss them altogether. If you're puzzled by what's happening to you in a foreign culture, it's probably the nonverbals that are causing the communication problem.

## Lecture Part 2:
## "Cross-cultural Misunderstandings"
**Mapping,** page 100

So, the nonverbals are probably responsible for most cross-cultural confusion. Let's see, let me give you one or two examples of how this can happen. A simple one is with eye contact. Americans tend to think that looking directly into another person's eye is appropriate, and that if you look away or you look down, you may be avoiding responsibility, or showing disrespect. And this is considered to be negative. We learn to "look me straight in the eye!" Look me straight in the eye. Now in some other cultures, it's a sign of disrespect to look at another person straight in the eye. In Japan, for example, there's much less direct eye contact than in the United States. So…something as simple as that can cause great confusion. To give another cross-cultural example from Japan, I can tell you that when I first began working in Japan, I was, oh boy, I was awfully confused because I was paying attention to what was said to me rather than to the nonverbal cues. We have a study-abroad program and when I was dealing with my Japanese colleagues, I would often ask questions, you know, that had to do with the program for our students. And I would ask one particular colleague if we could make certain changes. Now, I have great respect for this colleague, and I know that he wanted to cooperate. There were times when I would ask him things like, for instance, "Can we allow students in the dormitory to stay out later at night?" And often the response I would get verbally was that maybe we could do that, and I always interpreted this as a green light, as a strong possibility, because maybe for me verbally means "Maybe! Yes! Probably! Let's find a way!" After all, he hadn't said "no." What I didn't understand was that for my colleague, who didn't want to embarrass me by saying, saying, speaking the word "no" directly – which would be considered impolite in his culture – he was telling me "no" by saying "maybe" and giving me other cues with his body language, and I had to learn to recognize what those cues were. Well, can you imagine what they might be, for example? Well, I started to realize that it had to do with how he said maybe, it had to do with his tone: whether he said, "Well, maybe!" meaning "Maybe, yes!" or "Maybe," meaning "maybe not." It had to do, perhaps, whether he looked embarrassed, or whether he looked uncomfortable when he said that, or whether he seemed excited about the idea, or not. Or, or maybe how he, his posture, his body posture, how he held himself. I had to start observing those things. Now, I'll admit to you that it's still very difficult for me because I don't understand the nonverbal cues in Japanese society as well as I might understand them here in my own culture. But now I'm much more aware that I have to pay attention to them and that I have to learn to observe more carefully. And you know what? That's probably the most important lesson of nonverbal communication – that is, we have to pay attention, to observe closely, what is happening both in our own patterns of communication and in those of the people around us, and that this really deserves our study and our attention. I mean, it's not only extremely interesting, but it's so important if we want to understand the more hidden sides of communication.

## Chapter 6: Touch, Space, and Culture

### Lecture:
### "Nonverbal Communication: The Hidden Dimension of Communication"
**Before the Lecture**
**Listening for stress and intonation,** page 114

1. How much of those expressions are conveyed through <u>verbal</u> communication? More often than not, our intense emotions are conveyed <u>nonverbally</u>.

2. More often than not, our intense emotions are conveyed nonverbally through <u>gestures, body position, facial</u> expression, <u>vocal cues, eye contact, use of space, and touching</u>.

3. Imagine what would happen if you don't understand this bubble. What might you experience? Possibly <u>discomfort, irritation</u>, maybe even <u>anger</u>.

4. It could express <u>affection, anger, playfulness, control, status</u>.... These are just a few functions of touch.

5. In <u>some</u> cultures, it is common to see same-sex friends holding hands and embracing in public. This behavior is not interpreted as sexual. However, think about this behavior in some <u>other</u> cultures. Is it appropriate?

### Lecture Part 1:
### "Sarcasm and Proxemics"
**Summarizing what you have heard,** page 116

Today, we're going to start looking at nonverbal language. Nonverbal communication has often been referred to as the "hidden dimension" of communication. Sometimes this dimension is so subtle that we do not even recognize the ways it shapes what we're saying or how people interpret our meaning. In fact, when you think about it, think of some of the emotions that you express in everyday life, like happiness, joy, sadness, and anger, irritation. How much of those expressions are conveyed through <u>verbal</u> communication? More often than not, our intense emotions are conveyed <u>nonverbally</u> [slight pause] through <u>gestures, body position, facial</u>

expression, vocal cues, eye contact, use of space, and touching. OK. Now, let me make two points about how nonverbal communication functions. One is, sometimes when we communicate, it may only be through the nonverbal cues. The nonverbal gesture carries all our meaning. But, secondly, nonverbal cues also function to help us interpret the verbal message, and this is the point I want to focus on first – that nonverbal cues help interpret, a verbal message. Where we see this really in a very subtle way is through the use of humor and sarcasm. Y'know, in humor and sarcasm, the verbal message – y'know, what is actually said – is only a small part of the message. It's often the nonverbal cues that signal: "Hey, how's this message to be taken, seriously or not? I mean, do they really mean it, or are they joking?" Take, for example, when an American sees a new style of clothing which they may not like – how they might signal that they don't like it. Well, they might say, "Oh, that's a good look." Well, OK, now, if you're from a different culture, how do you know if they really mean it, or if they're being sarcastic, and they really mean the opposite? Well, it's very difficult because it's the nonverbal cues – not the words – that are carrying the meaning here. It's usually the tone of voice or a facial expression. I guess this is why a lot of international students often tell me that it's humor that's the most difficult part of American culture to understand. And similarly, when Americans go abroad. There's another area of nonverbal communication that is often overlooked, and in this case, the nonverbal gesture carries all the meaning – and that is proxemics. That's P-R-O-X-E-M-I-C-S. Proxemics refers to our personal space. Y'know, the anthropologist Edward Hall calls this personal space of ours our "body bubbles." Body bubbles are interesting because they're very subtle. You hardly ever recognize them until someone pops your bubble. In other words, when somebody comes too close, or violates your private space, you are suddenly conscious – you become conscious of the bubble. So, what do you do when somebody pops your bubble? Do you feel uncomfortable? Do you move away? Do you turn your position? Do you put your books in front of you? Do you suddenly close your jacket? We

always, we tend to adapt our body position when our bubbles get invaded. We see this in crowded elevators, for example. Body bubbles are influenced by many factors: How intimate is the relationship? What is the social context – a party or a bus? What is the gender relationship? However, a strong influence on body bubbles is culture. For example, in Latin American and Middle Eastern cultures, the kind of conversational space, the space between two people just engaged in everyday conversations, is relatively very close compared to Asian and American cultures. Imagine what would happen if you don't understand this bubble. What might you experience? Possibly discomfort, irritation, maybe even anger.

---

## Lecture, Part Two: "Touch"

### Summarizing what you have heard, page 117

And a third area of nonverbal communication, an area that's extremely powerful, where there are very strong norms – um, that's kind of social, unspoken social rules – strong norms that are easily violated is the area of touching. Touch is one of the most sensitive areas of nonverbal communication because touch is never neutral. Take the case of shaking hands with someone. We never think of shaking hands as a form of touch; it seems almost like a ritual. But, in fact, it's one of the major forms of touch between strangers. Now, in American culture, for example, we value firm handshakes. I mean, if the handshake is weak and limp, we might say, "He or she shakes hands like a fish." Touch is really amazing. It's very subtle and complex. Think for a moment about some of the functions of touch. What could it express? Well, it could express affection, anger, playfulness, control, status… . These are just a few functions of touch. Two major influences on touching behavior – think about your body bubbles again – one is gender, and the other is culture. We can see both influences – of gender and of culture – when we contrast same-sex touching – this'd be touching between two men or between two women. In some cultures, it is common to see same-sex friends holding hands and embracing in public. This behavior is not interpreted as sexual. However, think about this behavior in some other cultures. Is it appropriate? Could it be taboo? I recall my own surprise. I remember when I was visiting in China, and I would see young men holding hands in the streets, and young women, also. And at first, I was surprised, but I thought it was, y'know, very affectionate, very warm. So I decided that I was going to incorporate the same habit when I came back to the United States. So my sister and I started to hold hands in public. But we felt very awkward about it, and we stopped doing it. So you see the norms for touching are very powerful. They're easy to violate and, as I discovered, they're difficult to change. That is why it is very important to understand what is appropriate touch and what is taboo in another culture. Last, I think we have to remember that even misinterpretations and confusion in nonverbal communication don't always end in serious misinterpretations, or anger, or alienation. They're oftentimes the source of a lot of humor, a lot of laughter, and a lot of camaraderie between people of different cultures.

# Unit 4: Interpersonal Relationships
## Chapter 7: Friendship

### Lecture:
### "Looking at Friendship"
**Before the Lecture**
**Using morphology, context, and nonverbal cues to guess meaning,** page 137

1. But it's also rather subjective; friendship means very different things to different people.

2. As a therapist, I'm always thinking about a client's social network. Along with sleep patterns and appetite, this is an important indicator of a person's general functioning. When I work with a client who's suicidal, it's always critical to take into account that person's support systems, and, and by that, I'm talking about family and friends

3. You probably know of adults who consider themselves "loners" and say that they are content with that condition.

4. There can be a lot of pain involved with friendship – it's a risky business. When we make friends,

or try to make them, we become vulnerable to rejection. Each of us probably has a painful childhood memory of being cast aside by one friend in favor of another.

5. … you may have heard of the concept of the "overscheduled child" – who is always busy, always going off to piano lessons or football practice or ballet class.

### Lecture Part 1:
### "The Role of Friendship in Good Mental Health"
**Listening for specific information,** page 139

In some respects, friendship seems like a very straightforward topic – everyone wants friends; most of us have friends. But it's also rather subjective; friendship means very different things to different people. What I'll be focusing on today is the importance of friendship to me, as an individual and as a psychotherapist, and then on some ways in which friendship is challenged today. [pause] My first memory of consciously contemplating friendship was as a young boy – I was about six or seven years old – and I heard an old song on the radio – "People." "People who need people are the luckiest people in the world." And I remember thinking: Is that really true? Do we need people? And is it OK to need people? And, as I've gotten older, more and more, I tend to answer that question in the affirmative. As a therapist, I'm always thinking about a client's social network. Along with sleep patterns and appetite, this is an important indicator of a person's general functioning. When I work with a client who's suicidal, it's always critical to take into account that person's support systems, and, and by that, I'm talking about family and friends. Does that person feel supported in the world? Do they have meaningful connections? There are two reasons why I think about that, and the first one is … the person who does feel supported is much less likely to attempt suicide in the first place. Suicide is very often the manifestation of an abject sense of alienation. And second, if a person is suicidal, it's very important to hook them up with their support systems so that they can be monitored and, and kept safe. Someone without friends is almost certain to be depressed. You probably know of adults who consider themselves "loners" and say that they are content with that condition. My sense is that while that may in part be true, it's almost always the function of a defense mechanism. There can be a lot of pain involved with friendship – it's a risky business. When we make friends, or try to make them, we become vulnerable to rejection. Each of us probably has a painful childhood memory of being cast aside by one friend in favor of another. And that really hurts. Rejection by friends is especially painful for children. So, many loners, after repeated rejection, adapt by consciously deciding not to get close to anyone. It's easier that way, and it's less painful. In effect, they're saying, "If I tell you who I am, and you don't like who I am, that's all I got. So I don't want to take that chance. I don't want to let you know who I really am." And of course, it's impossible to form a friendship if you're isolating yourself from other people like this. To make friends you have to run the risk of being rejected.

## Lecture Part 2:
## "New Challenges to Friendship"
### Listening for specific information, page 141

I want to talk about some of the challenges to … friendship that I see in modern life today. One has its roots in childhood, which of course is when we learn how to make friends. There's been a lot of study recently of how contemporary life affects children – you may have heard of the concept of the "overscheduled child" – who is always busy, always going off to piano lessons or football practice or ballet class. Of course, activities are good, but children also need unstructured time – in a safe place, of course – where they can just "hang out" with their peers – without tasks or deadlines. It is in those moments that a child can really get to know another child, and that is the basis of developinglife-long friendships.

And of course, the pressures of modern life have an impact on adult friendships as well. Ask a friend today, "How are you?" and odds are the answer will be, "I'm so tired!" or "I'm much too busy!" or both. People spend more time at work, and the result is less quality time with family and friends. We may say that friendship is the most important thing in life, but that doesn't prevent us from moving across the country to take a better job if we have the opportunity.

Now this brings me to another aspect of modern life that may influence friendships – and one that I find extremely interesting and at the same time worrisome – and that has to do with the impact that social networking has had on … on the way in which people conduct their friendships. Facebook, instant messaging, texting, Twitter – these forms of communication are replacing to a great extent the kind of contact that friendships used to rely on – face-to-face interaction. Go to any café or public place and it seems like almost everyone is "wired" – they're using some kind of electronic means of communication – even if they are sitting with a group of friends.

I mentioned earlier how mobility – for example, moving across the country for a new job – how that presents a huge challenge if we're trying to maintain a friendship, and in the past, it would probably have spelled the end of the friendship. Well, clearly, Facebook, Skype, instant messaging, all of these tools make it possible now to maintain long-distance relationships. You may have people yourself that you stay in close touch with using one of these … tools.

But let's look again at these people texting in a café. We call this "social connectivity," and it's true that you can connect instantly with someone thousands of miles away, but it is not clear what the quality of that connection is – whether it can truly be called an intimate friendship.

I'm not saying these social-networking tools are bad – and I think they can be vital to sustaining an existing friendship. But as far as making new friends – well, think about this verb that we use on Facebook – "friending" … "to friend" - just how meaningful is it to say "I have 683 friends on Facebook!" Are they really friends?

In conclusion, in terms of human history, social networking is a relatively recent phenomenon, so… we do not know what impact it will have on the nature of friendship. But I think it is safe to assume that friendship will survive. We are by nature social animals, we all want and need people in our lives that accept us and love us for who we are. The people we love – and who love us back – are our friends.

## Chapter 8: Love

### Lecture:
### "Love: What's it all about?"

**Before the Lecture**
**Taking advantage of rhetorical questions,** page 156

1. Why do you fall in love with one person but not another person?
2. A lotta people might like a ten, but if you're a five, then who are you gonna end up getting married to?
3. If she graduated from graduate school, and he flunked outta kindergarten, do you think that relationship is gonna last very long?
4. Same age or about. Now, what's kinda the accepted age range?
5. Now, what about the idea that opposites attract?
6. You know that story of Romeo and Juliet?

**Taking advantage of rhetorical questions (continued),** page 156

1. Why do you fall in love with one person but not another person? Well, the sociobiology people, they would tend to say that you fall in love unconsciously, with somebody that's a good genetic match. Or something like that
2. A lotta people might like a ten, but if you're a five, then who are you gonna end up getting married to? Well, probably somebody closer to a five
3. If she graduated from graduate school, and he flunked outta kindergarten, do you think that relationship is gonna last very long? Probably not.
4. Same age or about. Now, what's kinda the accepted age range? Usually five to ten years, with exceptions, of course.
5. Now, what about the idea that opposites attract? And you've probably heard that, that's kinda the complementary theory, or complementarity.

6. You know that story of Romeo and Juliet? You know, their families hated each other, and they said, "You stay away from him!" "You stay away from her!"

---

### Lecture Part 1:
### "The Matching Hypothesis"
**Outlining practice,** page 158

This seems to be one of the more difficult topics to discuss. What is this thing called love? It seems everybody has a different idea about love. Why do you fall in love with one person but not another person? Well, the sociobiology people, they would tend to say that you fall in love unconsciously, with somebody that's a good genetic match. Or something like that. "Boy, she'd produce nice kids, so I love her!" Now, sometimes, women like guys that are tall, and muscular. Well, the sociobiologist would say that, well, they would produce a good, you know, gene pool. You know, that's why we like tall muscular types – or something like that. Now, even though you might like somebody – and you say, "Wow, she's beautiful – she's definitely a ten!" – you know, a lotta people might like a ten, but if you're a five, then who are you gonna end up getting married to? Well, probably somebody closer to a five. We tend to marry people like that, people that're like we are. We tend to really like people that're like we are. And that's homogeneity, or similarity. Some people call this the matching hypothesis – that we tend to be attracted to somebody that's like us. In fact, you're apt to stay married, too, if you married somebody that's like you are.

Of course, the matching part is more than just the physical. Maybe you've seen a couple walking down the street and said, "Wow, what is she doing with him?" Maybe she's a ten and he's a three, or something, or the other way around. And what that is, that's when you match up with someone, first, you notice the physical package, but then you start adding things in, like their personality, their job, their intelligence, and maybe when you look at the total, you might decide that they're a good match for you even if physically maybe they're not.

What else? Like, let's see, what'd be some things that …? One would be the same educational background. If she graduated from graduate school, and he flunked outta kindergarten, do you think that relationship is gonna last very long? Probably not. Like, for example, I recall one student in a four-year college – a long time ago – that she didn't go on to graduate school because she was afraid it would break up the marriage. And he'd only graduated from high school. She's graduated from college. And he kept bugging her about being a college graduate. "You're so smart! Why don't you do it!" Right? "Well, you're the college-educated one!" Y'know, that sorta thing. So, she didn't wanna have even more of a gap, so she actually stayed down, and you might say, 'cuz he didn't wanna go up. Now that's kinda too bad. So, we tend to marry somebody similar in education. Often you met 'em in school. What else should they be the same about? Uh, interests! You'd have about the same interests often. So, what else? Maybe the same values? OK. Same religion, maybe. Same race. Same age or about. Now, what's kinda the accepted age range? Usually five to ten years, with exceptions, of course. But usually within five to ten years. What else would there be? Socioeconomic status, age, education, race, religion, values, interests, things like that.

## Lecture Part 2:
## "The Matching Hypothesis (continued) and Other Theories"
**Outlining practice,** page 159

OK, so, generally the more similar you…are, the more apt you are to stay married. And that really works. But you might say, "Well, gee, Bob! I'm a guy who flunked kindergarten, and my wife has a graduate degree." Or, "My mom has a degree, and my dad never graduated high school." Or what? I dunno. "He's Catholic and she's Jewish," or "She's 23 and he's 42," or whatever it might be. And, "Hey, they've been doin' fine!" That could be. But, as a general rule, the more different you are in these, it just increases your probability of getting a divorce. We also tend to find people who have similar politics to what we have. If you're liberal, you'll tend to marry someone that's liberal. Or a conservative will marry a conservative 'cuz

you don't wanna marry someone that keeps telling you you're wrong. So, we also marry someone who sorta validates our ideas. We're kinda psychologically comfortable with those people. And, as I said, these marriages have a greater chance of lasting.

Now, what about the idea that opposites attract? And you've probably heard that, that's kinda the complementary theory, or complementarity. I dunno why it is academics try to make big words outta little words. Instead of the difference theory, y'know, they say the complementary theory or complementarity, or something like that. But anyway. Difference. Well, that can work for magnets. With people, difference is not, it doesn't work as well as similarity does, but it can be a factor. Like if one person is dominant, are they better off with another dominant person, or are they better off with a person that's more submissive, that likes people telling 'em what to do? Probably a dominant person is more apt to marry a submissive person. And maybe he or she likes the other person to be dominant and that works out OK. So, there is something to that. Probably two dominants don't work well, or maybe two submissives don't work well: "Whaddyou wanna do?" "I dunno, whatever. Whadda you wanna do?" "I dunno. Whatever." So, maybe, so probably won't work too well. But, in general, the research that we have says that people that marry someone that's like they are tend to stay together.

One other factor that can bring a couple together is called the "Romeo and Juliet effect." You know that story of Romeo and Juliet? You know, their families hated each other, and they said, "You stay away from him!" "You stay away from her!" So, what did Romeo and Juliet do? Yeah, they got married. So, the Romeo and Juliet theory says the more opposition you face to a relationship, from parents or friends, or whoever, the more attractive that relationship is to you. The more people say, "Don't! You shouldn't!" the more you wanna do it. Pretty interesting, huh? And it turns out these couples usually stay together, too.

So, those are some of the things that bring people together. And probably the most important thing to remember is the similarity idea – that we tend to be attracted to and happy with people who are like us.

# Appendix

| | | | |
|---|---|---|---|
| academic | conflict | gender | mentally |
| accommodate | consequence | grade | method |
| achieve | consume | grant | minimize |
| achievement | contact | hypothesis | misinterpret |
| adapt | contemporary | identify | misinterpretation |
| adult | context | identity | modify |
| adulthood | contrast | impact | monitor |
| affect | contribute | implication | mutual |
| alterable | convince | incidence | negative |
| alter | cooperate | incorporate | network |
| analyze | correspond | indicate | neutral |
| anticipate | couple | indicator | normal |
| appreciate | create | individual | normally |
| appropriate | cultural | inference | norm |
| approximately | culture | initially | obvious |
| area | data | injure | obviously |
| aspect | decade | insert | occur |
| assignment | defined | instance | odds |
| assume | definitely | institution | overseas |
| available | depress | intelligence | participated |
| aware | detective | intelligent | percent |
| bond | dimension | intense | percentage |
| capable | discrimination | interaction | period |
| challenge | document | interpret | phenomenal |
| chapter | dominant | investigation | phenomenon |
| chart | dramatic | involve | philosophical |
| chemical | economic | involvement | physical |
| circumstance | emphasis | isolate | physically |
| classical | energy | isolation | positive |
| colleague | enormous | issue | precede |
| commitment | environment | item | previous |
| commit | establish | job | primary |
| communicate | establishment | lecture | process |
| communication | estimate | lecturer | professionally |
| complement | ethic | liberal | professional |
| complementary | evidence | license | psychological |
| complex | expert | locate | psychologically |
| component | factor | maintain | psychologist |
| computer | final | major | psychology |
| concentrate | finally | maturation | range |
| concept | financial | mature | react |
| conclusion | flexible | mechanism | reaction |
| conduct | focus | medical | reject |
| confirmation | function | mental | rejection |

## Academic Word List vocabulary *continued*

| | | | |
|---|---|---|---|
| relax | seek | straightforward | theory |
| relaxation | series | stress | topic |
| relevant | sex | stressful | traditionally |
| reluctance | sexual | structure | unalterable |
| rely | sexually | style | unpredictable |
| remove | shift | summarize | unstructured |
| require | significant | survive | vary |
| research | similar | sustain | violate |
| resident | similarity | symbol | violation |
| resolve | source | task | vision |
| respond | specific | technically | |
| reveal | statistics | technique | |
| role | status | tense | |

# Skills Index

# Credits

## Text Credits

Page 6. Frequent signs of too much stress, stress and the immune system adapted from the brochure *Stress in College: What Everyone Should Know.* Copyright © 1996, with permission from American College Health Association.

Page 12. Pavlov's classical conditioning adapted from *The Oxford Companion to the Mind,* edited by Richard L. Gregory, Copyright © 1987 Oxford University Press, by permission of Oxford University Press.

Page 19. Findings from studies on stress and immunology summarized from *The University of California Berkeley Wellness Newsletter,* October 1993.

Page 21. Five prevention strategies adapted from http://www.mayoclinic.com/.

Page 73. Paragraph adapted from *Psychology: Being Human, Fourth Edition* by Zick Rubin and Elton B. McNeil, HarperCollins Publishers, 1985, p. 213. Reprinted with permission.

Page 119. Adapted from http://changingminds.org/explanations/behaviors/body_language/proxemics.htm. Used by permission of ChangingMinds.org.

Page 127. Excerpt from *Encounters* by Stephen Thayer, *Psychology Today,* March 1988, p. 36. Reprinted with permission from *Psychology Today* magazine, Copyright © 1988 Sussex Publishers , Inc.

Page 136. Information adapted from http://www.nytimes.com/2009/04/21/health/21well.html.

Page 161. Information adapted from http://www.associatedcontent.com/article/155259/five_reasons_why_people_marry_the_wrong.html?cat=41

## Illustration Credits

Page 43: David Benham

Page 47, 118: "Zits" used with the permission of the Zits Partnership, King Features Syndicate and the Cartoonist Group. All rights reserved.

Page 48: Eric Olson

Page 65: "Candorville" used with the permission of Darrin Bell, the Washington Post Writers Group and the Cartoonist Group. All rights reserved.

Page 79: "Dustin" used with the permission of the Steve Kelley, Jeff Parker, King Features Syndicate and the Cartoonist Group. All rights reserved.

Page 119: David Benham

Page 130 *(bottom)*, 159, 164: Rob Schuster

Page 141: ©ToonClipart.com

## Photography Credits

1 ©Cat London/iStockphoto; 3 ©Medioimages/Photodisc/Getty Images; 6 ©KidStock/Blend Images/Getty Images; 7 ©Jose Luis Pelaez Inc./Blend Images/Getty Images; 16 ©Steadman Productions; 21 ©Blend Images/ERproductions Ltd./Getty Images; 23 ©ZUMA Wire Service/Alamy; 24 ©uwe umstätter/imagebroker/Age Fotostock; 26 ©Jose Luis Pelaez Inc/Blend Images/Getty Images; 28 ©jedi-master/fotolia; 33 ©Chris Schmidt/iStockphoto; 36 ©Pali Rao/iStockphoto; 39 ©Steadman Productions; 45 ©Rob Lewine/Getty Images; 50 ©Anastassiya Andreyanova; 51 ©Mojgan Amidi; 57 ©Ted Streshinsky/TIME & LIFE Images/Getty Images; 62 ©Steadman Productions; 69 *(top to bottom)* ©Blue Jean Images/SuperStock; ©LWA/Dann Tardif/Blend Images/Getty Images; 72 ©Design Pics/SuperStock; 76 ©Steadman Productions; 85 ©AP Photo/Bernat Armangue; 87 ©Image Source/Getty Images; 88 *(clockwise from left to right)* ©PictureNet Corporation/Alamy; ©Alain Schroeder/Getty Images; ©iStockphoto/Thinkstock; ©Jose Luis Pelaez Inc./Blend Images/Getty Images; ©Shutterstock; ©AP Photo/Alastair Grant; ©Oppenheim Bernhard/Digital Vision/Getty Images; ©Michele Constantini/PhotoAlto Agency RF Collections/Getty Images; 89 ©Alfredo Estrella/AFP/Getty Images; 91 *(top to bottom)* ©Amanda Ahn/dbimages/Alamy; ©Topic Photo Agency/Age Fotostock; 92 ©Spotlight Photography; 96 ©Image Source/Getty Images; 101 ©Steadman Productions; 102 ©Manan Vatsyayana/AFP/Getty Images; 104 *(clockwise from left to right)* ©Simon Watson/Botanica/Getty Images; ©a-wrangler/iStock/Getty Images Plus/Getty Images; ©Chris Ryan/OJO Images Ltd./Alamy; ©AP Photo/Morry Gash; 107 ©Lane Oatey/Getty Images; 108 ©Yagi Studio/Digital Vision/Getty Images; 113 ©Steadman Productions; 122 ©Tracey Whitefoot/Alamy; 123 ©Manfred Rutz/Taxi/Getty Images; 125 ©Laurence Mouton/PhotoAlto/Getty Images; 127 ©Stockbroker/Alamy; 130 *(top to bottom)* ©Christina Krutz/Masterfile; 133 ©Rachel Watson/Digital Vision/Getty Images; 134 ©Andrew Bret Wallis/Photodisc/Getty Images; 135 ©ZUMA Wire Service/Alamy; 139 ©Valueline/Punchstock; 140 ©Steadman Productions; 143 ©Look and Learn/Bridgeman Art Library; 145 ©BananaStock/Punchstock; 148 ©moodboard/Cultura/Getty Images; 151 *(top to bottom)* ©DAJ/amana images inc/Alamy; ©Paul Burns/Lifesize/Getty Images; 155 ©Steadman Productions; 157 ©MIXA/Getty Images; 165 ©Datacraft Co Ltd./Getty Images